WORD
BIBLICAL
THEMES

General Editor
David A. Hubbard

Old Testament Editor
John D. W. Watts

New Testament Editor
Ralph P. Martin

WORD
BIBLICAL
THEMES

1,2 Thessalonians

LEON MORRIS

WORD PUBLISHING
Dallas · London · Sydney · Singapore

1, 2 THESSALONIANS

Word Biblical Themes

Quotations from the Scriptures in this volume are the author's own translation unless otherwise indicated.

Library of Congress Cataloging-in-Publication Data

Morris, Leon, 1914–
   1, 2 Thessalonians / Leon Morris.
     p. cm.—(Word Biblical themes)
   Bibliography: p.
   Includes index.
   1. Bible. N.T. Thessalonians—Criticism, interpretation, etc.
I. Title. II. Title: First, Second Thessalonians. III. Series.
BS2725.2.M67 1989
227'.8106—dc19   89-5632
                                   CIP

ISBN 0-8499-0797-7

9 8 0 1 2 3 9 RRD 9 8 7 6 5 4 3 2 1

Printed in the United States of America

CONTENTS

EDITORS' FOREWORD

The two Pauline letters to the church of the Thessalonians have the distinction of being among the first pieces of extant correspondence between the apostle and his congregations. They offer the modern reader a wonderfully descriptive and appealing case history of early Christianity, set in Greco-Roman society and beset by pressing problems of a doctrinal and ethical character. They also reveal Paul's handling of those issues and the way he expected infant believers, only recently won over from Hellenistic religious culture, to adopt the Christian way of belief and behavior.

For Christians in our day, living as we do in a society which has lost a lot of the familiar landmarks of traditional doctrine and ethical standards, these short letters have a particular appeal.

Dr. Leon Morris of Melbourne, Australia, is no newcomer to the field of biblical exposition. In fact, he may be regarded as a veteran in this area, having produced an impressive array of commentaries and studies on New Testament life and literature. Nor is he unacquainted with the Thessalonian letters, since he has already released two volumes, in previous series, on these epistles.

The Word Biblical Themes project, which aims to make the results of scholarly study readily accessible to lay people and ministers of the word, is fortunate to have secured his consent and cooperation in writing the following small book. Students will still value Professor F. F. Bruce's erudite contribution to the Word Biblical Commentary on the Thessalonian epistles (vol. 45; hereafter referred to in the text as WBC 45); to a wider audience, Dr. Morris's distillation of theological themes carries all the marks of his own reflection and will prove a valuable companion volume and one to be used in its own right.

The University of Sheffield
Department of Biblical Studies
England

Ralph P. Martin
New Testament Editor
Word Biblical Themes

PREFACE

I count it a privilege to have been invited to write the Word Biblical Themes book on the Thessalonian Epistles. The series is a significant one, with its emphasis not so much on the critical questions as on the theological ideas of the letters and their permanent message for believers.

There is a particular significance in studying the Thessalonian correspondence because the two letters to the church in Thessalonica must have been written by about A.D. 50. Most people hold them to have been the earliest letters of the great apostle (although some think Galatians was earlier). Whatever opinion may be favored on that question, there seems little doubt that these letters were written less than twenty years after the crucifixion. It is fascinating to see how many of the great Christian doctrines had already made their appearance by that time.

The Thessalonian church had no great history of earlier believers to inspire them such as we have with our stories of great Christians throughout the ages. We learn a good deal about these early believers from what Paul says, and we find that they have much to teach us. They made their mistakes, and there was much that they did not understand, but they stood firm in difficult circumstances. Of course, the counsel the great apostle gave them is still full of interest and inspiration to Christian people. We can all profit from a close study of the great ideas expounded in these two letters.

Leon Morris
Melbourne, Australia

INTRODUCTION

Thessalonica was situated at the head of the Thermaic Gulf (now called the Gulf of Salonika), with a fine harbor in front of it and a fertile plain behind it. These facts, taken with the additional fact that the *Via Egnatia*, the main highway from Rome to places east, passed through it, meant that the city was an important trading center (as it still is). It was the capital of the Roman province of Macedonia and its largest city.

Paul came to this city on his second missionary journey. Together with Silas and Timothy he had preached at Philippi, but he and Silas had been put in jail, and on their release they had left that city (Acts 16:40). When he came to Thessalonica Paul went to the synagogue, according to his custom. He preached there on three (apparently successive) sabbaths (Acts 17:2). This might mean that his stay in the city was something just short of a month, in which case he engaged in a short, intense campaign. This is not impossible, although most people hold that when he was no longer welcome in the synagogue, Paul preached elsewhere in the city for a further period, so that he may have been there for several months.

Abraham J. Malherbe thinks that Paul continued to evangelize, perhaps using Jason's home as his base. He draws attention to the *insula*, a type of apartment house frequently found in first-century cities, which "would contain a row of shops on the ground floor, facing the street, and provide living accommodations for the owners and their families over the shop or in the rear." They would also have "living quarters for visitors, employees, and servants or slaves."[1] Jason, who "received" Paul and his company (Acts 17:7), was apparently well-to-do, and he may well have been the proprietor of such an *insula*. If so, it would have provided lodgings for the preachers, a place where they could earn their living (1 Thess 2:9), and a base for their evangelistic work. Whether this was what happened or not, we do not know. What we do know is that Paul centered his preaching on the necessity for the Christ to suffer and rise and on the fact that Jesus is the Christ (Acts 17:3).

The result was a number of conversions from among the Jews, together with "a great multitude of the devout Greeks and no small number of the chief women" (Acts 17:4). This success, however, aroused opposition led by some Thessalonian Jews (doubtless angry at losing some of their adherents), and there was a riot. Unable to find Paul, angry men dragged Jason, Paul's host, and other believers before the city authorities. They gave a notable description of the preachers as "These that have turned the world upside down" (KJV) and complained that they were acting against Caesar's decrees (Acts 17:6-7). The authorities took "security" from Jason and the others, then let them go (Acts 17:9). Luke does not say what form this security took, but it would seem that Jason and the others agreed to keep the peace.

The riot and subsequent events made it impossible for Paul and his companions to continue with their mission in Thessalonica, so the new believers sent them off by night (Acts 17:10; this points to continuing danger and a need for secrecy). Now the new little church was left to build up its life without the presence of its founders. Paul had been with them for only a short period. Whether we see that period as a few weeks or a few months, it might seem all too short a time for firmly establishing a new church. Thus, being on their own was quite a test for the new believers. There was no long history of the Christian church and not many examples for the fledgling church to appeal to, and they had not had the time or the opportunity to be given instruction in all aspects of Christian teaching.

That the church did stand firm is made clear from Paul's subsequent history. He went on to Berea, where his preaching resulted in conversions (Acts 17:12), but Thessalonian Jews followed him and stirred up such opposition that he had to leave. He went on to the intellectual center of Athens, a city where some believed but where Paul was mocked and where his successes were apparently limited. That meant that the apostle had had setbacks in four successive cities. In Philippi, Thessalonica, and Berea, some very promising beginnings had been ended when fanatical opponents had run him out of town, and he was ridiculed in Athens. Small wonder, then, that when he got to Corinth he described himself as "in weakness and in fear and in much trembling" (1 Cor 2:3; J. B. Phillips renders, "I was feeling far from strong, I was nervous and rather shaky"). A very human Paul was clearly a very discouraged man at this point in his career.

We do not have a full account of the travels of Silas and Timothy, but Luke tells us that they were left at Berea when Paul went to Athens, that Paul asked for them to come to him as soon as possible (Acts 17:14–15), and that they came to him in Corinth (Acts 18:5). This account is not complete because

Paul was left in Athens alone when he sent Timothy to Thessalonica (1 Thess 3:1-2). In due course Timothy came back to him (1 Thess 3:6), which probably means that he reached Paul in Corinth. A return to him in Athens does not allow sufficient time for the faith of the Thessalonians to be known "in every place" (1 Thess 1:8) and for them to have come to need the kind of advice he gives in 1 Thessalonians.

The important point is that when Timothy brought him news of the situation in Thessalonica, Paul could see that his work had not been in vain. He had been driven out of the city before he had wanted to go, but that did not mean that he had failed. Clearly the church had been firmly established in Thessalonica, and God had set his seal on the work his servant had done. So Paul wrote out of a full heart to a church that was dear to him.

Problems facing the new church

Timothy's report had shown clearly that on the whole the church was in good shape, but there were some problem areas, and Paul wrote to help his friends deal with the difficulties that confronted them. It is plain that there was still fierce Jewish opposition, in which a principal feature apparently was strong criticism of Paul, which he rebuts vigorously (1 Thess 2:3-8). There was some form of persecution from pagans (1 Thess 2:14), and, of course, in a pagan city there was always a temptation to go back to the low moral standards of those among whom the believers lived (1 Thess 4:4-8). An interesting problem arose from Paul's teaching about the Second Coming. Some of the believers seem to have held that this would take place very quickly, and when some of their number died, they thought that these fellow believers would lose their place in the glory (1 Thess 4:13-18). The time of Christ's return is, of course, not known to believers, and Paul had to say something about this (1 Thess 5:1-11).

A curious feature is that some of the new believers had ceased to work for their living, with the result that they depended on the generosity of others who did work, and Paul gave instruction about how to treat them (1 Thess 5:14-15). Additionally, as has happened all too often in the history of the church, some of the rank and file did not see eye to eye with their leaders (1 Thess 5:12-13). Then there were those who did not agree with others about the work of the Spirit (1 Thess 5:19-20). The apostle did not lack interesting topics on which to write.

It is clear that Paul wrote not long after Timothy made his report (1 Thess 3:6; cf. 2:17), and this, in turn, was not long after the church was founded. As, however, the faith of the Thessalonians was widely known (1 Thess 1:8), we must allow for a few months to have elapsed. Putting all this together most scholars think that the first letter is to be dated about A.D. 50, which makes it one of the earliest of Paul's letters, perhaps the earliest. Galatians may have been earlier, but no other letter of Paul's can predate these two, at least none among those that have survived.

Paul the Pastor

This early letter reveals to us Paul the pastor as he deals with the problems that have arisen and strives to bring his converts the insight they need as they go forward into the largely uncharted path of Christian service. The letter lacks a detailed treatment of the great doctrines of the faith that we find in some of his other letters, but its early date and the glimpse it gives us of Paul at work meeting the needs of enthusiastic but as yet imperfectly instructed believers makes it very important for our understanding of the early church. In this letter we are also able to see some of the problems that arose in the first days of the church and how those problems were met. The result is a moving document

5

and one of permanent importance for the Christian church.

A second letter

Then there came a second letter. There are some scholars who hold that 2 Thessalonians was not written by Paul but by an imitator. They find a combination of likenesses to 1 Thessalonians and differences from it and feel that, on the one hand, Paul would not have repeated himself so closely and, on the other, that, for example, the eschatology undergirding the two letters is mutually incompatible. In the first letter it is said that the Second Coming is expected soon and will occur suddenly, while in the second it will be preceded by signs, specifically the appearance of the Man of Lawlessness. They think also that there is a difference in tone, with the first letter being much warmer and more friendly than the second. For these reasons, they think it likely that 2 Thessalonians was not written by Paul but by someone at a later date who imitated him, but whose different ideas and more distant approach betray him.

Against this it is fairly argued that the resemblance passages are too close. The ideas, the style, and the vocabulary are all Pauline. The imitator must have thought with the very mind of Paul! The differences in eschatology are difficult to take seriously because it is part of the nature of the apocalyptic form to embrace variety. Specifically, many apocalypses combine the thoughts that there will be signs before the coming of the End and that the End will come suddenly and unexpectedly. As for the difference in tone, that is largely subjective. The difference is not as apparent to some readers as it is to others, and in any case it is asking too much that any writer should always write in the same tone. Writers have their dismal moments as well as their brighter days.

Another view is that Paul was joined in writing one or both letters by either Silas or Timothy, and that his colleague contributed the major share. If either wrote both letters, we are up against the same problems as if Paul wrote them. If Paul wrote the first letter and Silas or Timothy the second, we have the problem of accounting for the close similarity of much of the language. There is also the fact that Paul signed the second letter (2 Thess 3:17), so he must have agreed with all that is written there. F. F. Bruce reminds us that Silvanus was one of the "leading men among the brothers" (Acts 15:22) and thinks that he may well have played a responsible part in the composition of the letters (WBC 45:xxxii–xxxiv).

While we cannot say that all scholars see Paul as the author of both letters, we can at least point to a respectable majority that take this view. None of the objections is without an answer, and in view of the express claim of the letter itself and of its suitability to the Thessalonian situation as we know it, it seems best to see 2 Thessalonians also as a genuine writing of the great apostle.

Different recipients?

If we cannot speak of different authors, some scholars are prepared to think of different recipients. The great German scholar Adolf von Harnack thought that in the Thessalonian church there were both Jews and Gentiles and that these were so divided that Paul sent two letters, one for each section. He thought that 1 Thessalonians was addressed to the Gentile section and 2 Thessalonians to the Jewish Christians. He could point to the reference to turning from idols (1 Thess 1:9) as suitable for Gentiles, but the Jewish coloring he saw in the second letter has not been apparent to most people.

A second argument depends on the fact that where traditionally scholars have accepted the reading "God chose you from the beginning" in 2 Thess 2:13, some very respectable textual authorities read "God chose you as a firstfruit" (accepted by GNB, Moffatt, etc.). The logic of this argument was based on the observation that the Thessalonians were not Paul's first converts nor were they the first converts in Macedonia; however, the first Christians in Thessalonica were Jews. Thus, if this reading of the Greek is accepted, it would make sense for the second letter to be addressed to Jewish believers.

In the first place, this puts a lot of stress on a variant reading. It is not at all certain that "firstfruit" is correct, and many see the other reading as much more probable (as RSV, NIV, etc.). In the second, it is impossible to see Paul acquiescing in a situation where one of his churches was so hopelessly divided that separate letters had to be sent to the two parts. His attitude to division comes out in his sharp words in 1 Cor 1:11–17, where he deferred dealing with anything else in his letter until he had roundly condemned the cliques that had sprung up in the Corinthian church. "Has Christ been parceled up?" he asks, "Was Paul crucified for you?" Why should such a man meekly send separate letters to two groups of Christians who were so much at odds that they would not meet together? Such a procedure for Paul would have been incredible.

Other factors also militate against such a view. The addressees of the two letters are practically identical; there is no indication that the letters were sent to different groups. A passage which is seen as meant for the Gentile part of the church (1 Thess 2:13–16) commends the readers for following the example of the churches in Judea. This does not seem likely if they did not see themselves as at one with local Jewish believers. This view must be mentioned when we are discussing 2 Thessalonians, but it has little to commend it and much that is against it.

A better suggestion is that of E. Earle Ellis, that 2 Thessalonians is addressed to church leaders, "Paul's Thessalonian co-workers."[2] Even this suggestion comes up against the fact that the addressees are such that the two letters seem to be sent to the same people.

Reversal of order

Some students think that we have the two letters in the usual order only because 1 Thessalonians is the longer and thus the church put it first. They hold that there are good reasons for thinking that what we call 2 Thessalonians was written first, and when we see this, we find some of our problems solved. Thus, they maintain, the troubles that beset the Thessalonians are at their height in 2 Thessalonians but seem to be in the past in the other letter. Similarly the difficulties within the church are said to be something that the writer has only just heard of in 2 Thessalonians but are familiar to him in 1 Thessalonians. Such arguments are subjective and they have not convinced very many. Nor is the contention valid that the reference to Paul's own signature (2 Thess 3:17) would be required in a first letter but not in a second. If this were accepted, it would be a reason for rejecting most of the Pauline correspondence in the New Testament; most of Paul's letters are first letters to churches and lack a reference to a signature.

Although the position is sometimes argued with great earnestness, it must surely be rejected. The problems Paul deals with—such as the Second Coming, the idlers, the persecutions—all seem to have progressed when we move from 1 to 2 Thessalonians. The references to another letter in 2 Thessalonians (2:2, 15; 3:17) seem to point to 1 Thessalonians (unless we think of a lost letter, for which there is no other evidence). There are personal reminiscences in 1 Thessalonians that are natural in a first letter but not nearly so natural if this was a follow up to a letter already dispatched.

9

All in all the idea does not commend itself. In the end we are left with the conviction that there was more behind the arrangement of these letters than the question of length. The early church evidently had good reason for placing 1 Thessalonians first, and we do well to follow those believers.

Why the second letter?

The question then arises, Why did Paul write a second letter so soon after the first and covering so much of the same ground? The answer appears to be that reports which came to Paul from Thessalonica showed that many of the same problems continued. The second letter contains no defense of Paul's conduct like that in the first, so Paul probably felt that that part of what he wrote had accomplished its purpose. Nevertheless, there were still some uncertainties about the Second Coming, some people were still idle, some disheartened. So Paul wrote once more to inform and inspire. The first letter had not accomplished all that he had hoped? Very well; he would send a second. This is the letter of a pastor determined to do what is necessary to meet the needs of those for whom he cared.

than 528 times. The entire New Testament uses the word 1,314 times; thus, Paul's use of the word is disproportionately greater than that of his fellow writers. In fact the apostle employs the term in more than 40 percent of its occurrences. The Pauline writings comprise no more than 24 percent of the total; hence, we see that the apostle uses the word "God" nearly twice as often as we might expect. Throughout the Pauline writings the word occurs on the average about once every 60 words. The word occurs 36 times in 1 Thessalonians and 18 times in the second letter. Statistics can be as dull as ditch water, but at least these figures make it abundantly clear that Paul is very interested indeed in God, in who he is and what he does. Whatever he is writing about, he relates to God.

God's love brings salvation

Such a concentration on God might conceivably arise from a religion of fear. We may be so afraid of a stern and judgmental Supreme Being that we spend a lot of time finding out what arouses the divine wrath and what worshipers must do to avoid that wrath. That is not Paul's way. Paul is certainly aware of the sterner side of God (and we shall come back to this later), but he is swept off his feet by the fact that the God who might be expected to be stern with sinners, or at best indifferent to them, proves instead to be a loving and considerate God.

He directs both letters "to the church of Thessalonians in God the Father" (1 Thess 1:1; 2 Thess 1:1; the second has "God our Father"). It is unusual to read of being "in" God (though cf. Eph 3:9; Col 3:3); Paul's habit is to speak of being "in" Christ. The new life Christians have, however, is a life in close fellowship with God, and this means that God in his love and in his mercy allows them to live in this close fellowship. It accords with this that Paul goes on to speak of "our

1   THE LIVING AND TRUE GOD

"You turned to God from the idols," writes Paul, "to serve God, living and true" (1 Thess 1:9). He thus draws attention to a major shift that had taken place in the lives and religious experiences of the Thessalonian Christians. They had formerly been adherents of the idols, who are here lumped together as one undifferentiated mass of falsity and pretense. Idol worshipers may distinguish between one and another, but for Paul there was no great difference. They were all false, all purporting to be gods and failing, all promising much and delivering nothing, all drawing devotion and service from devout worshipers and leaving them empty. By contrast the believers had turned to the one God. In contrast to the idols, he is living whereas they are no more than inanimate objects of wood and stone. He is the true God where the idols are no more than shams.

It is unsurprising, then, that early in his letter Paul speaks of one's relationship to God and sees this as central in the process of conversion, for Paul is a God-intoxicated man. In the Pauline corpus we find the word *theos*, "God," no less

God and Father" (1 Thess 1:3), a typically Christian way of speaking. Jews might well use Paul's words about the "living and true" God (1 Thess 1:9), but they did not place an emphasis on God as Father to the extent that Paul and other Christians did. They used the term, of course, but for them it was not typical and for Christians it was.

Two short prayers inserted into the argument are instructive (1 Thess 3:11–13; 2 Thess 2:16–17). In both Paul links Christ with the Father, which tells us something of what he thought about his Savior. In both he calls God "Father" and speaks of him as active in the lives of his children. Thus the Father (together with Christ) will "direct our way to you" (1 Thess 3:11): Paul looks to the Father to be active in the work that the missionaries are doing and thus in promoting the well-being of the converts. The believers should then "abound in love," and their hearts are to be strengthened "blameless in holiness before our God and Father at the coming of our Lord Jesus with all his holy ones" (vv 12–13). God is not remote and uncaring. He is deeply concerned about his people. He is active in bringing about their growth in Christian qualities, and his concern and his activity will persist to the end.

The second prayer is directed to Christ and to "God our Father who loved us and gave eternal encouragement and good hope in grace" (2 Thess 2:16). There is some discussion as to whether we should see the love and the gift as emanating from both Christ and the Father, but there is certainly no doubt that the Father's love is spoken of and his activity is seen in encouraging his people. Yet another prayer is that the Lord may direct the converts' hearts "into the love of God" (2 Thess 3:5). Grammatically this could mean direct them to love God, and this would agree with Paul's general use of the expression "the love of God." In this context, however, it is more likely that it is God's love for the believers that is in mind. In any case their love will always be a

13

response to God's prior love. Whichever way we choose to interpret the love of God, it is important to see that the Father does not look on believers with lofty detachment but rather with love. So it is that Paul can call the Thessalonians "brothers beloved by God" (1 Thess 1:4).

Paul can also speak of "the churches of God" (2 Thess 1:4). Just as the churches are "in" God, so they belong to God. Paul does not think of the churches as no more than assemblies of like-minded people. They are assemblies of people who belong to God, and the assemblies as such belong to God. This, of course, tells us that God is interested enough in believers to have them as his own.

God brings salvation

The love of God brings people to salvation. Throughout these letters it is clear that our salvation does not rest on our own efforts: salvation is the gift of God. Thus "God chose you from the beginning (or, as a firstfruit) for salvation . . . unto which also he called you" (2 Thess 2:13–14). The initiative in salvation does not come from the sinner but from God. Moreover, God is "the God of peace" (1 Thess 5:23), which points to the same thing. He does not acquiesce in a state of affairs wherein sinners rebel against his just order. He takes the initiative to bring them back to himself, to restore the peace that had been disrupted by sin. References to grace underline the point (2 Thess 1:12; 2:16; and the salutations and farewells in both letters), for grace always means the absence of merit in the recipient and the bountiful generosity of God who gives.

"God did not appoint us for wrath but for the obtaining of salvation through our Lord Jesus Christ" (1 Thess 5:9). The wrath of God is a reality insisted upon in Scripture, and we must not shut our eyes to its grim reality. Those who are saved are not saved from some imaginary trouble but from a very real disaster. Thus, Paul exults that God's purpose for believers is not eternal loss: God's purpose is salvation. At this point the apostle does not spell out all that salvation means, but its opposition to "wrath" demonstrates that he has in mind a positive blessing in the presence of God.

This is also involved in the references to "the gospel of God" (1 Thess 2:2, 8, 9). The very idea of "gospel," with its good news of what God has done to bring about the salvation of sinners, points us to the love and graciousness of God, but this is emphasized when the gospel is specifically said to be "of God." "Of" may mean that the gospel is peculiarly God's or that it originates from God. Both are true and both are important.

There is a similar idea involved when Paul speaks of the way the message he and his friends preached had been received. It is not easy to translate his words, but he says something like this: "Having accepted the word of hearing [i.e., the word you heard] from us of God [this awkward sequence puts emphasis on 'of God'] you received not the word of men but as it is truly the word of God" (1 Thess 2:13). However difficult it is to find a precise English equivalent for an unusual Greek passage, the meaning is clear. Paul is saying emphatically that when the gospel was preached in Thessalonica, his hearers had accepted what the preachers said, not as a piece of interesting human wisdom, but as the very word of God. That is the important thing. The gospel is God's word, not a human invention.

The God who calls

The divine initiative may also be brought out with the idea of 'call,' an important part of Pauline theology. It is not expressed as frequently in the Thessalonian correspondence as in some of Paul's letters, but it is interesting to see it in these early writings. For Paul it is clear that people do not become

Christians because on the whole they believe it is a good idea. They become Christians because God calls them, calls them out of their self-centered existence, calls them into a life of fellowship and service.[1]

So Paul says that God did not call us for impurity but in sanctification (1 Thess 4:7); he prays that believers will be deemed worthy of their call (2 Thess 1:11) and reminds his readers that he had taught them "that you should walk worthily of the God who calls you into his own kingdom and glory" (1 Thess 2:12). Paul often uses walking as a metaphor for the steady (if unspectacular) progress that should characterize the Christian. His emphasis here is on the way the call of God issues in changed lives. Changed lives are important, but we should notice that it all begins with the divine call. In this passage Paul uses the present tense, which may be used to tell us that God is "the calling one," the God who calls. Or it may remind us that, while it is true that God has called us once and for all, it is also true that God is constantly calling. As Mrs. C. F. Alexander expressed it,

Day by day His sweet voice soundeth,
Saying, "Christian, follow Me."

The present tense is used again when we learn that "Faithful is he who calls you" (1 Thess 5:24; cf. Rom 8:30; 1 Cor 1:9). Once more there is the thought that it is characteristic of God to call people, he is "the calling one." This time there is also the thought that the calling one is thoroughly reliable. Long ago Abraham had said, "Shall not the Judge of all the earth do right?" (Gen 18:25), and the thought here too is that God may be relied upon. He will not let his people down. Paul adds "who also will do": God is not only a caller but a doer. The Greek has no "it" (though, of course, it is implied), and the simple expression "will do" places its emphasis on the divine activity. God not only calls but also sees through to its completion what that call implies (cf. Num 23:19; Phil 1:6).

The same basic thought is brought out from another angle when Paul writes, "he called you through our gospel" (2 Thess 2:14). The past tense directs attention backward to the time when the little band of preachers had visited Thessalonica and the voice of God made itself heard through what they said. The gospel directs our attention to the good news of what God has done for our salvation, and a call that is effected through the gospel is another way of saying that it is God who has called believers out of their former way of life, called them through the good news of what he has done for their salvation in Jesus Christ. That the gospel is "our gospel" does not mean that Paul is claiming any part in originating the salvation to which "gospel" points. It means that this is the message that he and his fellow workers preach, a message that they have fully appropriated so that they have made it their own. They have experienced its power, and when they preach it, they preach it with conviction. It is now "their" gospel as well as being in a different and fuller sense God's.

God defeats evil

There is a stern passage early in 2 Thessalonians in which Paul makes it clear that God is implacably opposed to evil and that in the end he will entirely overthrow it. This is both a warning to believers to avoid every evil thing and an encouragement to them. No matter how powerful evil appears to be, its power is limited and its final overthrow certain.

The section about evil begins with the surprising statement for believers patiently undergoing persecutions and afflictions that all this is "a demonstration of the righteous judgment of God" (2 Thess 1:5). It is, of course, not so much the sufferings themselves that demonstrate God's righteous judgment as the bearing of the believers as they experienced this evil. Paul and his colleagues boasted about the Thessalonians among the churches of God "on account of your steadfastness and faith in all your persecutions and the afflictions that you endured" (v 4). That they reacted in this way demonstrates that God was at work. It is a righteous thing that God enables his servants to react to unmerited suffering and persecution like this.

We should also bear in mind that the attitude of the first Christians toward suffering was not always identical with ours. We often see suffering as an unmitigated evil, and we do everything we can to avoid it. We rarely stop to reflect that suffering, rightly borne, develops character, or that we are appointed to suffer (1 Thess 3:3). Suffering is an inescapable part of life and one that can be valuable. Our faith is not meant to be some fragile thing that must be kept in a kind of spiritual cotton wool packing. It is to be robust and well able to face the turmoil and the troubles of life in our day. When we find our need abundantly supplied so that we are able to remain calm and steadfast in the middle of life's agonies, we have evidence of God's "righteous judgment" (2 Thess 1:5) as did the Thessalonian Christians. We do not fully discern that judgment when we see it only in the punishment of those we regard as wicked. This righteous judgment is evident when God's people remain constant in a fallen world that brings suffering on all, with no escape for either good or bad.

One of the things that puzzles believers is the way evil people prosper and succeed in many of their aims. It was the problem with which Job wrestled agonizingly and which has never been solved to human satisfaction. One relevant factor, however, is the belief that evil will be punished eventually, and Paul goes on to bring this out. It is "righteous" (or

"just") for God to recompense evildoers. Specifically, those who afflict the Thessalonian Christians will one day experience affliction themselves (2 Thess 1:6). Evildoers must expect to experience the wrath of God (Rom 1:18ff.). The verb "recompense" suggests the idea of paying what is due. Paul is saying that justice demands that those who do wrong should suffer for it and, in the end, they will do so.

That he is looking forward to judgment day comes out in the following words. Suffering believers will enjoy "rest with us," Paul says, "in the revelation of the Lord Jesus from heaven with his angels of power" (2 Thess 1:7). Those who do not know God and do not obey the gospel are singled out as the future recipients of "eternal destruction from the face of the Lord" (vv 8-9). The knowledge of God may be spoken of as eternal life (John 17:3), and here we are confronted with the opposite. Paul is not writing about a vengeful God but pointing out that those who reject the gospel and choose to live without God must in the end bear the consequences of their choice.

There is a startling expression of this in the later statement about those who "did not receive the love of the truth so that they should be saved." Paul says "for this reason God sends them a working of delusion so that they believe the lie" (2 Thess 2:10-11). Modern Christians find it difficult to ascribe such an act to God; we find it easier to think that evil people bring about their own delusions. The Bible, Old Testament as well as New, however, sees God as completely sovereign so that he works out his purpose through the evil that people do as well as through their good deeds. This is a moral universe, and God has made it so. He made this world such that "the wrath of men" will praise him (Ps 76:10). The Book of Job makes it clear that Satan acts only within limits that God allows. Paul assures us that God "gives up" evildoers to the consequences of their sin (Rom 1:24, 26, 28). When

19

the wicked receive the due consequences of their deeds we are not to think that this is something which takes place quite apart from God. We are not to forget either that "God has shut up all men to disobedience, so that he may have mercy on all" (Rom 11:32). Even when he deals with the disobedient and evil, God's ultimate purpose is mercy.

All this should be borne in mind, but at this point our interest is basically in the fact that evil will not go unpunished. The Thessalonian correspondence makes it clear that God is just and, therefore, he will in due course punish evil as well as bring believers into eternal felicity. Moreover, we should be clear that this is the working out of justice (2 Thess 2:12), not vengeance. Even the Man of Lawlessness, with all his blasphemous evil and all his awesome power, will be destroyed (2 Thess 2:8); nothing and no one can ultimately escape the judgment and the justice of God.

Elsewhere Paul speaks of the danger of believers acting "in lustful passion even as also the Gentiles who do not know God" (1 Thess 4:5). This is not innocent ignorance but the kind of thing Paul has in mind elsewhere when he refers to Gentiles "who did not approve to have God in knowledge" (Rom 1:28). There and here he is referring to culpable ignorance and to a danger inherent in this situation. Believers who ought to know better may be seduced into the same kind of conduct as the Gentiles. He warns them that "the Lord is the avenger of all such" (1 Thess 4:6). Again we see that evil is punished.

In two instances Paul calls God to witness (1 Thess 2:5, 10). On both occasions he is referring to the absence of bad deeds or the presence of good ones, but for our present purpose the important thing is that God takes notice of what people do. The God of whom Paul writes is witness of the deeds that we do and of those that we refuse to do. This has its relevance for those who break his laws and walk in the ways of evil.

We have seen that God has taken the initiative in bringing salvation; it is his call that initiates the whole process, and it is the good news of what he has done in Christ that provides the way of forgiveness. We should not think, however, that God is simply a God who cleans up the mess after people have sinned. He does indeed provide a wonderful atonement for our past misdeeds, but he also looks to those whose sins have been put away to live lives that match their forgiveness. The Thessalonian correspondence makes it abundantly clear that God is interested in the way believers live out their faith and that he provides for them.

"This is the will of God, your sanctification" (1 Thess 4:3). In context, the particular emphasis is on sexual purity. Paul is drawing attention to the laxity that was so characteristic of Gentiles generally and making the point that believers must not be led astray by this bad example. In such a situation it is easy to take it for granted that the way of the Gentiles is the accepted way of life. For believers, however, this is not the accepted way of life. The lives of believers are not to be governed by the general level of morality in the community in which they find themselves, but by what God wills them to be and to do. Paul does not refer to any one specific command of God, as he might well have done. He chooses rather to draw attention to the will of God.

Believers, of course, notice the way other people live, but when it is a matter of imitation they must choose their models carefully, as part of the service of God. Paul commends his readers for being imitators of the churches in Judea in Christ; the same sufferings made their appearance in both and were borne in the right spirit (1 Thess 2:14). Early in the first letter Paul tells the Thessalonian Christians that their faith in God is spoken of "in every place" (1 Thess 1:8). They had profited from good examples before

God and had themselves become patterns for other Christians.

When he delivers people from the consequences of their sins, God wills for them that they should live in the best way of all. In the passage just noted we see that this involves sexual purity, but, of course, it involves a great deal more. The will of God applies across the whole range of Christian living. Paul's immediate subject is the importance of chastity, but he says a good deal more when he says that the will of God is "your sanctification." This is a comprehensive word, wide enough to cover the whole of life. In other words, while Paul is dealing with one particular evil, his warning directs attention to the fact that God is interested in the way believers live throughout the whole of life.

The apostle is aware that not everyone accepts this view. He takes notice of people who reject or disregard the injunction to sanctification and says that they reject "not man but God" (1 Thess 4:8). The command he has given is not simply one that comes from the best human wisdom: Paul is telling them what God has laid down as the way his servants should live. Again we have the thought that God is interested in all of life and that it is he and not some lesser being who sets standards for believers.

Paul uses the expression "this is the will of God" again (5:18). This time it is immediately linked with the giving of thanks, but thanksgiving is the third of three activities in this passage: "Rejoice always, pray incessantly, in everything give thanks." We should take the reference to the will of God to cover all three. The Christian life is a life of rejoicing, and not only on pleasant days. It is clear throughout this correspondence that the Thessalonian believers were going through tough times. Paul was not directing a conventional exhortation to people who lived on easy street; he was writing to people who were in trouble and who he knew were in trouble. In that context he says "Rejoice always." The source of the joy of Christians is not to be found in the circumstances in which they find themselves but in what God has done for them and continues to do for them. Out of that joy and that spiritual communion proceeds a sense of constant prayer ("Prayer is the Christian's vital breath"), and from constant prayer one finds a spirit of thanksgiving.

The apostle has set an example for his readers by beginning his letter with a statement of thanksgiving for the Thessalonian believers, assuring them that he and his friends remember them constantly in their prayers (1 Thess 1:2). He interrupts his argument to tell them again that he gives thanks for them (1 Thess 2:13) and again to ask rhetorically what thanksgiving he can render to God for all the joy the Thessalonians have given him (1 Thess 3:9). He regards thanksgiving as something he "ought" to do (2 Thess 1:3; 2:13); it is not simply an option for people who like that sort of thing. Notice further that Paul's rejoicing on account of the Thessalonians is a rejoicing before God (1 Thess 3:9). He is not writing about some form of worldly exhilaration but about a spiritual joy that takes note of the presence of God and is a joy that is part and parcel of living in the service of God. We are all wrong if we think of the Christian way as a grim path along which we must give away all the things we like. It is full of wonderful things for which we should be giving constant thanks.

Some people try to live the Christian life like they pay their taxes. Nobody likes paying taxes. When the time comes, we search high and low for every exemption we may lawfully claim. We reduce the amount to the lowest total we can and then pay, grimly hoping that when the tax auditor is through we will have enough left over on which to live. It is possible to have a similar mentality in spiritual things. There are people who see God as something of a kill-joy, constantly making demands that his people give up this or that. They build

The Living and True God

themselves up to making the sacrifice and hope that when it's done there will be enough left to make life bearable.

This is a caricature of the Christian way. The God we serve is a God of joy as well as a God who sets before his own the highest of standards. Those who serve him rightly do so not in a spirit of grim resignation but rather one of joy. Joy before God is an integral part of being Christian. The Thessalonian letters have a good deal to say about the joy Paul felt over his converts, and this is not despite God's demands but a joy in the presence of God. Paul speaks of "all the joy with which we rejoice on your account before our God" (1 Thess 3:9), and he calls on the Thessalonians to rejoice always (1 Thess 5:16). He reminds them that despite their many troubles when they were evangelized they received the word "with joy of the Holy Spirit" (1 Thess 1:6). The Thessalonian Christians were themselves the joy of the apostle (1 Thess 2:19, 20). It thus does not surprise us that he boasted about them in the churches of God (2 Thess 1:4).

Worthy of God

Another way of emphasizing the importance of believers living in the right way is brought out with the exhortation "that you should walk worthily of the God who calls you into his own kingdom and glory" (1 Thess 2:12). We have already noticed the importance of this passage for what it teaches us about the divine call. Now we see that it also tells us something very important about the kind of life which those who are called must live. As we said earlier, Paul often uses the metaphor of walking for the Christian life; it points to the unspectacular but constant progress that the Christian should be making. For our present purpose, however, the adverb "worthily" is the significant word. Christians know that their own merit does not bring about their salvation. Salvation is due to God alone. Since Paul's readers are being saved, it is important that they live lives that befit their new station. Here Paul sets the standard as high as it is possible to set it. They are to walk "worthily of God"; there can be no higher standard than that.

Sometimes the idea is given that God approves of people, as when Paul says, "We have been approved by God to be entrusted with the gospel" (1 Thess 2:4). His verb "approved" strictly means "approved by test" and there may be the thought that God had tested his servants before trusting them to preach the gospel. Whether this is Paul's intent or not, there is no doubting that God is concerned that the gospel be preached and that the messengers to whom he entrusts it should be fitting preachers.

In accord with this emphasis on fitness for the service of God, the Thessalonians are to "walk" in such a way as to please God (1 Thess 4:1). We have seen that God witnesses all that believers do, and they should bear this in mind and live constantly in such a way that everything they do will be right in his sight and please him. Paul maintains that he and his associates were approved by God to be entrusted with the gospel and that, accordingly, they do not speak like people who are trying to please their audiences. Their purpose is to please God. Paul brings out the seriousness of this matter by saying that God "tests our hearts" (1 Thess 2:4). By contrast, those who persecute the church "do not please God" (1 Thess 2:15; he adds, "and are contrary to all men"). Paul is not laying on his converts the responsibility of doing something he was not prepared to do himself. He set out to do what was pleasing to God, and he looked to them to do the same.

We are not far away from this when we find that the preachers "were bold in our God to speak God's gospel to you amid much conflict" (1 Thess 2:2). He refers to the fact that he and his friends had been insulted and mistreated in Philippi, but he does not say (as many would probably say)

25   The Living and True God

that when they came to Thessalonica they were more circumspect and made sure that they kept themselves out of trouble. That might be the way of the world, but the missionaries had been entrusted with God's gospel, and, because it was God's, they must proclaim that gospel faithfully, no matter what the cost to themselves. *God's* gospel must be taken to the ends of the earth.

These letters have a good deal to say about the end of the age and the wonderful events that will then transpire. Much of this concerns our Lord Jesus, and we will be looking at this teaching in another section. Here it is appropriate that we should take notice of the fact that God is linked with these great events. We read that the Lord will come down from heaven with a shout, with the voice of the archangel "and with the trumpet of God" (1 Thess 4:16). Paul does not say who will blow this trumpet or precisely what the sounding of the trumpet signifies, but the way he mentions it shows that God is active in initiating the events of the great day.

He also tells us that, along with Jesus, "God will bring those who have fallen asleep through Jesus" (1 Thess 4:14). This means that we must see God as active at the time of Jesus' return. It is easy to be so taken up with the coming of our Lord that we overlook the fact that the Father is just as much involved in those events as is his Son. We look to the Father to see to it that the dead in Christ will rise and that they will be with him.

2   JESUS CHRIST OUR LORD

In modern times Christians often refer to their Savior simply as "Christ," a habit that we largely owe to Paul. The word "Christ" is the translation into Greek of the Hebrew word that means "anointed." In English we transliterate both, and thus we get the two words "Christ" (from the Greek) and "Messiah" (from the Hebrew); both signify "anointed." Among the Hebrews in the Old Testament there were many "anointed ones." The term is most frequently used of the king, especially in the expression "the Lord's anointed" (e.g., 1 Sam 24:10). At times we read of "the anointed priest" (Lev 4:3) and now and then a prophet was anointed (1 Kgs 19:16). The anointing was a solemn mark of consecration: the anointed one was set apart to serve God in some special way.

There were many "anointed ones," but over the years the expectation grew that in due course God would send not just *an* anointed one, but *the* anointed one, someone who would do his will in a special way. This one would be greater in his own person and greater in the work that he would do

27

than all the others. The actual word "Messiah" is not often used of him in the Old Testament, but that the Messiah would come in due course was widely believed.

This messianic hope seems to have burned brighter at some times than at others. Not surprisingly, people looked for the Messiah with special eagerness at times when the nation was in deep trouble. People searched the Scriptures for passages that would tell them something about this anointed one (cf. John 1:45). According to Alfred Edersheim, the rabbis found 456 Old Testament passages that should be understood of the Messiah (Edersheim lists the verses and quotes rabbinic passages where they are discussed[1]). Some of these Old Testament passages were doubtless not understood to refer to the Messiah until some time later than the New Testament, but clearly there were many that were understood in this way from quite early days.

Thus when Paul referred to Jesus as "the Christ" he was using a term that would arouse significant associations in all those familiar with the Jewish Scriptures and the discussions that arose from these writings. Sometimes this expression is used as a title, but this is rare in Thessalonians (possibly in 1 Thess 3:2; 2 Thess 3:5). Paul uses "Christ" so often and in such ways (e.g., in letters addressed to Gentiles where the title would be meaningless) that, to all intents and purposes, it has become for him a proper name. That is the way we normally use it today.

The term "Christ" occurs in the Pauline writings 379 times out of a New Testament total of 529, so that Paul has more than 70 percent of the total number of references. He uses it as many as 65 times in a single letter (Romans), whereas it is found no more than 25 times in any non-Pauline writing (viz., Acts, which is much longer than any Pauline letter). We see from all this that no other New Testament writer remotely approaches Paul in his frequent use of the word; "Christ" is a Pauline word. It is to this apostle that we owe our habit of referring to Jesus by this name.

The word occurs ten times in each of the Thessalonian letters, which is not as frequent as in some of the other Pauline writings, but it is still a substantial number. The apostle uses the name "Jesus" sixteen times in 1 Thessalonians and thirteen in the second letter. Thus, in this correspondence, it is the human name "Jesus" that is preferred (overall Paul uses this name 213 times; the most in any one of his writings is 37 in Romans; by contrast, in John's Gospel it is found 237 times).

He also uses "Christ" a respectable number of times, but in these two letters he uses "Lord" more than either, twenty-four times in the first letter and twenty-two times in the second. With this total of ninety-five uses for the three expressions, we see that in the Thessalonian letters Paul speaks often of the Savior who had come to mean so much to them.

"Lord," of course, is not a name but a title. It was used in a variety of ways, for example, of the owner of possessions (e.g., Matt 20:8), and thus of the owner of slaves (e.g., Luke 14:21). It was not, however, confined to owners of anything; the term could be used as a form of respectful address in polite society, much like our "sir" (e.g., John 12:21). It was a word that must have been often on the lips of people in the first-century Roman Empire.

In religious usage it came to signify much more than a polite form of address. For example, in the Septuagint (the Greek translation of the Hebrew Old Testament) it is characteristically used to render "Yahweh," the name of God. It was also common in other religions, and pagans often referred to their deity as "Lord." In the Roman Empire it was applied as well to the emperor and sometimes expressed the thought of his "divinity." It is unlikely that Paul derived his usage from pagan sources and much more probable that he was taking over the usage of the Septuagint and giving to Jesus the title customarily used of Yahweh. Of course, when he used it in speaking or writing to pagans, or people who had been pagans, he would not have been unmindful that it was an exalted and meaningful title for them too. When Paul uses this term of Jesus, he is putting him in the highest place. It is not unlikely that sometimes Paul uses "Lord" to refer to God the Father, following Old Testament usage, but this is not frequent. Characteristically when he says "Lord," he means Jesus.

In some places he uses one of these expressions, the name "Jesus," or "Christ," or "Lord," but quite often he combines them. In these letters his favorite combination is "Lord Jesus Christ," mostly in the form of "our Lord Jesus Christ." This combination occurs fourteen times in these two letters, and the form "Lord Jesus" occurs ten times. When he combines "Jesus" and "Christ," he prefers the order "Christ Jesus," which he uses seventy-three times in his letters (twice in Thessalonians), while "Jesus Christ" is found eighteen times (not at all in Thessalonians; in a number of other passages there is such variation in the manuscripts that it is impossible to be sure of the original order). There does not seem to be any significance in the order; it is just the way Paul speaks. Interestingly, when he includes "Lord," the order is usually "Lord Jesus Christ" (forty-nine times) rather than "Lord Christ Jesus" (eight times).

Jesus and God

Paul does not say anywhere, in precisely these words, "Jesus is God," and many modern scholars find this significant. They feel that the apostle deliberately avoided attributing deity to Jesus and assume that he saw Jesus as less than fully divine. That he never says "Jesus is God" is clear, but that he does not see Jesus as fully divine is more than difficult to reconcile with some of the things he actually does say.

Thus he addresses both letters, as we noted earlier, to "the church of Thessalonians in God the Father and Lord Jesus Christ" (1 Thess 1:1; 2 Thess 1:1; the latter has "our Father"). It is not easy to see how any created being, anyone less than God, could be linked with God the Father in such a way. Clearly Paul put Jesus in the highest possible place. We see this also in the fact that in the same passages the church is said to be "in" the Lord Jesus Christ as well as "in God the Father." The church is "in" Christ in the same sense as it is "in" the Father; the one "in" covers both. How can the Thessalonian church be "in" the Lord Jesus Christ if he is no more than a first-century Jew? Especially as the churches in Judea are also "in" him (1 Thess 2:14). Although "in" may be considered a somewhat elastic word and the precise meaning in these passages difficult to bring to expression, it is not easy to see how a merely human Jesus could have a number of churches, so widely separated, "in" him.

We might say a similar thing about the greeting that is so much a feature of any Pauline letter, "grace and peace to you" (1 Thess 1:1; 2 Thess 1:2). In the second letter the grace and peace in question are expressly said to be "from" God and Christ, and the same origin of these qualities is implied in the first. If, on the one hand, Christ is in some sense one with God, then there is no great problem in seeing him as the bringer of such qualities to believers. If, on the other, he is no more than a man, how can he bring grace and peace to anyone? This is not a casual expression because the association of grace with Jesus is repeated (5:28; 2 Thess 3:18; it is linked with the Father and the Son in 2 Thess 1:12; 2:16). The connection with the opening salutations and the closing greetings is, of course, found throughout the Pauline correspondence. It was habitual to the great apostle to link grace with the Lord Jesus.

In both letters there is a prayer near the middle. In the first letter Paul speaks of "God himself and our Father and our Lord Jesus" and asks them to direct the path of Paul and his companions to the Thessalonians. It goes on to pray that "the Lord" will make the Thessalonians abound in love toward one another and toward all people and that he will confirm their hearts blameless before God the Father at the coming of our Lord Jesus (1 Thess 3:11-13). In the second letter the corresponding opening refers to "our Lord Jesus Christ himself and God our Father" and seeks that the hearts of the Thessalonians be encouraged and that they be strengthened in every good work and word (2 Thess 2:16-17). To some it is breathtaking to find Christ not only linked with the Father but placed first (cf. 2 Cor 13:13; Gal 1:1). To others the order is of very little significance.

Whatever we think of the order in which they are mentioned, clearly in such passages the Father and the Lord Jesus are closely linked indeed, and the reversal of order in the second prayer may be held to give expression to this. William Neil commented, "The only theological significance to be attached to the variations in order is that there is complete equality in the apostle's mind between the Father and the Son. It is only through his knowledge of Christ that he has come really to know God. For him they are One."[2]

F. F. Bruce cites the first part of this passage and expresses his agreement: "With this we may agree, bearing in mind that for Paul the equality was one of purpose and action rather than a metaphysical equality" (WBC 45:196). It is not easy to know whether Paul distinguished between "equality of purpose and action," on the one hand, and "metaphysical equality," on the other. If he did, then this is the way to put it. We must, however, also go on to ask whether what he says means anything less than metaphysical equality. We should also add that the church speedily affirmed the metaphysical equality, and this came to expression in the creedal statements of the early church. It is not easy to see how another prayer, "the Lord be with you all" (2 Thess 3:16), is to be understood without seeing the Lord as sharing in the nature of the Father.

This may be in mind also when Paul says that God has called his Thessalonian correspondents "into his own kingdom and glory" (1 Thess 2:12). So, too, God called them "into the acquiring of the glory of our Lord Jesus Christ" (2 Thess 2:14). Thus the final glory into which believers are called may be spoken of as God's glory or as Christ's glory. It is plain that in Paul's mind the two are not separated: he can speak indifferently of either as the one to whom the glory pertains.

At the end of the first letter Paul writes "I adjure you by the Lord that . . ." (1 Thess 5:27), that is, "I put you on oath by the Lord . . . ." It is not impossible that he would invoke an oath by a created being, but it is more likely that we should see this passage as another indication of the stature of the Lord as Paul saw him, as one who is to be ranked with the Father rather than simply with humans. This is the implication of a passage in which Paul brings out a stern side to Christ's activity. Paul warns the Thessalonians to beware of committing a certain sin and adds, "because the Lord is the punisher concerning all these things" (1 Thess 4:6). With this we should take the reference to his punishing those "who refuse to know God and who disobey the gospel" (2 Thess 1:8). Paul is in no doubt as to the greatness of his Lord.

From another point of view the greatness of the Lord Jesus is brought out when Paul writes, "you know what commands we gave you through the Lord Jesus" (1 Thess 4:2). He does not detail the commands at this point, but clearly he has in mind the Christian tradition that goes back to Jesus himself. "Through the Lord Jesus" may mean that the commands in question originated with God the Father and that they came to the apostles "through" Jesus. Or it may signify something like "in the the name of the Lord Jesus." Another suggestion is that the preachers spoke as people in touch with the Lord Jesus. It is a difficult and unusual expression, but whichever way we take this phrase it is plain that for Paul the immediate origin of these commands is the Lord Jesus and, further, that he sees them as significant. They are not to be shrugged off as though they were optional advice. Because they came through Jesus they are of continuing relevance. Jesus is not to be thought of simply as a man who died some years before, but as Lord of their lives. His commands still matter.

Similarly, Paul can "command you, brothers, in the name of our Lord Jesus Christ" (2 Thess 3:6), and he can "command and exhort in the Lord Jesus Christ" (2 Thess 3:12). The "name," of course, in some way sums up the whole person, and both passages indicate that definite orders which are linked with Jesus can be given. Somewhat less authoritatively Paul says, "For the rest then, brothers, we request and exhort you in the Lord Jesus . . ." (1 Thess 4:1). Although he comes short of issuing a command in this passage, a request and an exhortation "in the Lord Jesus" must obviously be given due heed. Paul is aware that what he is doing is something done in Christ. As he puts it elsewhere, he is sure that he has "the mind of Christ" (1 Cor 2:16), and the requests he makes proceed from this standpoint. Both he and the Thessalonians are "in" Christ, and what Paul says must be understood in accordance with this.

It is from this point of view that the Lord Jesus is to be seen as directing believers along their Christian way. It is "the Lord" to whom Paul looks to "direct your hearts into the love of God and into the steadfastness of Christ" (2 Thess 3:5). "The love of God" might mean God's love for his people or his people's love for God. In Paul the former meaning is almost invariable, but we need not think the other is excluded. After all, our love for God is always an answering love: he first loved us, and it is this prior love of God that evokes our love for him. We should probably take "the steadfastness of Christ" in much the same way. Undoubtedly Paul is reminding his readers of the steadfastness that Christ showed in very trying circumstances. Yet he is also praying that a steadfastness like that may make its appearance in his friends in Thessalonica. He is not urging them to pull themselves together to produce this desirable quality out of their own resources. He is praying that the Lord will produce it in them. Again we see Paul looking for Christ to do something that is quite impossible in one who was no more than a man.

The same thing is to be seen in prayers such as those we have already noticed that link Christ with the Father. We gave attention to the implications of the link between the two, but we should also bear in mind that it is highly unusual to have anyone linked with the Father in prayers like those in these letters: prayers that the preachers' way should bring them to Thessalonica again, that the Lord should increase the love of the converts for one another and for other people, and that their hearts should be strengthened so that they be blameless at the coming of the Lord (1 Thess 3:11-13). It is similarly significant that the Lord Jesus Christ should be asked, along with the Father, to encourage the hearts of the converts and to strengthen them in every good work and word (2 Thess 2:16-17). How can a created being answer prayers like these?

We should add to this the petition that "the Lord of peace" should give peace to the converts (2 Thess 3:16). The expression is found only here in the New Testament, but we find "the God of peace" elsewhere (Rom 15:33; 16:20; 2 Cor 13:11; Phil 4:9; 1 Thess 5:23; Heb 13:20). As "the Lord" in Paul almost invariably means Jesus Christ, there is no reason to doubt that this is his meaning here. It is significant that he uses an expression that resembles so strongly a recurring way of speaking of the Father and, further, that he looks to the Lord Jesus to bring peace to the believers at all times and in every place.

With this we should take the fact that the first letter links faith, love, and hope and that the last-mentioned is the "hope of our Lord Jesus Christ before our God and Father" (1 Thess 1:3). It is possible that the Greek should be taken to link faith and love with the Lord Jesus and not only hope. The sentence construction, however, favors the link with hope and so does the strong eschatological emphasis in the letter as a whole. Either way, Jesus is assigned a very special place.

We should not overlook the fact that in referring to the divine will for his correspondents Paul calls it "the will of God in Christ Jesus" (1 Thess 5:18). That the will of God should be "in" Christ Jesus is yet another indication of the greatness of Jesus as Paul understood things divine. Jesus is not like an angel, a submissive being who does the will of God. He is one in whom that will resides. We may or may not be able to understand how the divine will relates to the Father and the Son, but there is no denying that Paul sees Jesus' place as central.

In this early correspondence we do not have a full account of the way Jesus brings salvation, although we should notice that "brothers beloved by the Lord" (2 Thess 2:13) points us to the mainspring of that salvation. It was because the Lord loved them so much that he brought about their deliverance from the sin into which they slipped so easily. Doubtless Paul's thought on this deepened and developed with the passing of the years (we must bear in mind that what we have in these letters was written less than twenty years after the crucifixion), but a more likely reason for the absence of a full discussion of the way salvation was wrought is that it was not needed for the purposes of the Thessalonian letters. There were other problems that troubled the Thessalonians, and Paul confines himself to dealing with these.

Even here Paul makes it clear that "God did not appoint us to wrath but to the acquiring of salvation through our Lord Jesus Christ" (1 Thess 5:9). Without specifically relating the death of Jesus to salvation, he says that the Jews killed the Lord Jesus (1 Thess 2:15). He later connects this with the love of God and of Christ. In a prayer that links the two, he speaks of him "who loved us and gave us eternal encouragement and good hope in grace" (2 Thess 2:16). The verb "loved" is most probably to be linked with both the Father and the Son, and the aorist tense should be noted. A. L. Moore can say, "The aorist tense probably indicates that Paul is thinking of the event in which this love was supremely displayed, the crucifixion of Christ (cf. Gal 2:20 'who loved me and gave himself for me' . . .)."[3] Paul certainly has this in mind when he speaks of awaiting God's Son, "whom he raised from the dead" (1 Thess 1:10), and again when he says, "if we believe that Jesus died and rose . . ." (1 Thess 4:14). There is no developed theory of the atonement in such passages, but plainly there is the deep conviction that the death and the resurrection of Jesus are important and that they bring about our salvation.

In an earlier section we saw that the gospel is sometimes "the gospel of God"; it is also "the gospel of Christ" (1 Thess 3:2) and "the gospel of our Lord Jesus" (2 Thess 1:8). This gospel is doubtless his gospel because it tells of what he did to bring about salvation. Central to the gospel is the truth that Jesus Christ died on the cross to bring about the forgiveness of sinners; thus, the gospel is his in a very special sense. It is his also in the sense that this is the message he gave his followers to proclaim in his name.

Incidental references

Next we should note a series of more or less incidental references to the Lord that bring out something of Paul's

37

view of his Savior. For example, he says that he and his companions might have been "burdensome as apostles of Christ" (1 Thess 2:6). He sees himself first and foremost as an apostle "of Christ": his commission is a commission from Christ, and he was content to order all the rest of his life in accordance with that commission. Further, Christ was such that when he sent apostles they could make demands on people. They would naturally receive sustenance from believers, no matter how burdensome that was.

Again he says, "we request and exhort you in the Lord Jesus" (1 Thess 4:1); the simple matter of making a request to the converts was done "in" the Lord Jesus. It was part of the way the lordship of Jesus covered the whole of life. It covered death, too, because Paul speaks of "the dead in Christ" (1 Thess 4:16). Even death, which seems to us to sever all ties, cannot sever the tie with Christ. In death, as in life, believers are "in Christ."

Paul not only has confidence in the Thessalonians, but he has confidence in them "in the Lord" (2 Thess 3:4). The local church leaders are "those who labor among you and are over you in the Lord" (1 Thess 5:12), while the rank and file will encourage Paul if they "stand fast in the Lord" (1 Thess 3:8). Both the leaders and the led are "in the Lord," which points to his superlative excellence. In such passages as these the apostle is not pursuing the theme of the lordship of Christ. They come in at a variety of points in the letters, and their incidental character shows us something of the place that Paul assigned to the Lord.

He refers to "the word of the Lord" with which we might compare "the word of God" (1 Thess 2:13). "This we say in the word of the Lord," he writes (1 Thess 4:15), thus making the Lord central to his preaching. Furthermore, he speaks of "the word of the Lord" as having gone out from the Thessalonians (1 Thess 1:8), so that they had experience of the same thing. When they set out to proclaim the Christian message they did not set forth some profound piece of Thessalonian wisdom that they had thought up for themselves; they proclaimed "the word of the Lord."

There is a very lively piece of imagery when Paul asks his friends to pray for him "that the word of the Lord may run and be glorified" (2 Thess 3:1). This is the same imagery as we see in Ps 147:15, where God's word "runs swiftly." There had been some spectacular results when the word had first been preached in Thessalonica with the consequence that the church had been firmly founded there. Paul is now looking for the word of the Lord to have a similar speedy effect elsewhere. Obviously he is not expecting a "word" by itself to do anything; it is "the word of the Lord" that matters.

Throughout this section we have been concerned with a series of statements Paul has made or questions he has asked or instructions he has given. Yet he is not discussing the person of Christ, and we look in vain for any section we might conceivably label, "What Paul thinks about Jesus Christ." These letters are not doctrinal treatises setting out theological truth with all the qualifications and provisos that are necessary to guard oneself from straying into error. They are simply the apostle's reaction to the situation at Thessalonica as he knew it. His converts were desperately immature, and they were on their own in a world violently opposed to many of the things they and Paul held most dear. They needed advice and encouragement, and that is what Paul is giving them.

What he says about Jesus when he is concerned to meet the needs of his converts in a troubled situation, however, enables us to see something of the way he saw his Savior. He certainly knew him as a man of Galilee; there is nothing docetic about Paul's view, nothing which would deny or qualify his humanity. Equally certain, though, he did not believe that ordinary human categories adequately described Jesus. Throughout this section, at point after point, we have

Jesus Christ Our Lord

seen how Paul ascribes to Jesus activities that we cannot help but see as pointing to a being greater than any human. Perhaps this is nowhere seen as plainly as when the apostle is writing about the happenings at the last great day. There is so much said on this topic, however, that it must have a section all to itself. Here we simply notice that throughout this correspondence Jesus Christ is consistently portrayed as one surpassing all human categories, one who must be thought of in the same way in which we think of God.

3   THE LAST THINGS

Quite a large proportion of these two letters is given to teaching about the Second Coming of Jesus to this earth, the end of life as we know it now and the ushering in of the final state of affairs. Paul had given teaching on these things when he was in Thessalonica, and he can write, "Do you not remember that when I was with you I told you these things?" (2 Thess 2:5). Part of our problem as we approach this section of our study is that we do not know just what it was that Paul had told them when he was with them. It is not difficult for us to gather that some Thessalonians had misunderstood what Paul had taught them and that part of the apostle's motivation to write was to correct this misunderstanding. We do not know exactly what they had misunderstood, and in all our discussions we labor under the handicap that we have no information about the things that Paul had taught them about which there was no problem. We must, therefore, maintain a reverent reserve. It is appropriate, of course, that we should give full weight to what Paul says, but it is also necessary for us to remember that there was much that is important to this subject of the Second Coming which Paul does not mention because it was not the subject of misunderstanding or misinterpretation.

The dead in Christ

Let us start with what was evidently quite a problem to some of the Thessalonians, the plight of believers who had died. From what the apostle says it would seem that some of the new believers had understood him to say that all believers would have their part in the great events that would take place when Christ comes back to this earth at the end of the age. After the apostle left them, some of their number died. These people would accordingly not be there to welcome the returning Lord and that apparently seemed to some Thessalonian believers to mean that they would miss the glory and the joy of that great day. Because they also seem to have believed that that day was not far off, they may well have thought this a great tragedy. For want of living only a short time longer, their friends had lost their part in the most wonderful day of all. What a tragedy!

Paul sets himself to help them. He introduces what he has to say with, "We do not wish you to be ignorant, brothers" (1 Thess 4:13), a formula he uses a number of times (Rom 1:13; 1 Cor 10:1, etc.). Mostly it seems to lead up to some new, important teaching. Each time he uses it, Paul addresses his readers as "brothers"; he is telling them something new, but he does so in an affectionate way, not in any spirit of superiority.

He is writing about those who "fall asleep." It is significant that throughout the New Testament this is the way the deaths of believers are reported. For those in Christ the sting has been taken from death; it is now only a matter of falling asleep. The other side of this is that this way of speaking is never used when the death of Jesus is reported. He did not "fall asleep"; he "died." He underwent the full horror of death, and because he did those who put their trust in him will never know that horror. They simply fall asleep and awake in the presence of God.

With this understanding as his starting point, Paul can say he does not want his readers to sorrow "even as also the rest who do not have hope." This sweeping characterization of the non-Christian world is not without justification. It would not be true to say that the pagan world of the first century unanimously viewed death as a horror; there were some who held that there would be an afterlife and there were some who took the thought of death quite calmly. Indeed, pagan writers often used "sleep" as a euphemism for death.

Those who viewed death calmly, however, were few. There is no evidence that the common people ever regarded death as no more terrifying than sleep. There can be no doubt that as a whole the pagan world of the first century had no hope when it contemplated death. Death was the end of all real life, and, if there was some form of life after death, it was seen as a shadowy existence in a Hades of some sort and far from the full-blooded life of the here and now. Significantly, the deceased were often called "shades." The gloomy inscriptions on the magnificent tombs of the wealthy pagans form a strong contrast with the utterances of hope scratched over the resting places of humble believers. Bruce cites Catullus:

> The sun can set and rise again
> But once our brief light sets
> There is one unending night to be slept through.

He also cites Theocritus: "hopes are for the living; the dead are without hope" (WBC 45:96).

Such statements demonstrate that Paul is not writing about a commonplace view of death that can be applied to all the race. He is talking about the difference that Christ's saving work has made. The salvation Christ won for believers has many aspects. One important distinction is that salvation has transformed the Christian's understanding of death (cf. 1 Cor 15:55). We see this when Paul goes on to say, "those who sleep through Jesus, God will bring with him" (1 Thess 4:14). "Sleep through Jesus" is a most unusual expression, and its precise meaning has been the subject of debate. Our best understanding of the words is that the people in question were believers; they were "in" Jesus at the time of their death. It is their relationship with him that has made their death different from the death of those outside Christ. The New English Bible paraphrases, but brings out the meaning, with "died as Christians."

The coming of the Lord

Having made it clear that deceased believers will be there when Jesus comes back to this earth, Paul goes on to further details of that coming. Perhaps we should notice in passing that our expression "the Second Coming" is not found in the New Testament; there we read simply of "the coming." Paul prefaces what he has to say on this subject with, "For this we say to you in the word of the Lord" (1 Thess 4:15); that is, he is not giving a private opinion. Speaking "in the word of the Lord" surely means that what he now says has the full authority of Jesus behind it. The words he quotes are not found anywhere in our canonical Gospels, but there must have been many sayings of Jesus that circulated orally in the early church (see Acts 20:35). Another suggestion is that the words come from a revelation made to Paul or to a Christian prophet. The precise means by which the saying came to the apostle is not important. What matters is that it had the full authority of Jesus behind it, so that Paul could cite it as giving teaching that the followers of Jesus must accept.

Paul goes on to say, "we who are alive, who remain at the coming of the Lord." This has led many to the view that Paul thought and taught that he would be alive when Jesus returns. Such people commonly see this as a widespread view of the early church. Both opinions may be correct. In every age of the church there have been some believers who held firmly that the Lord would be returning in their lifetime. There is no reason why there should not have been many such in the first century or even that Paul may have been included among them.

We cannot, however, deduce this from anything Paul said. The words just quoted certainly do not teach as much. Long ago J. B. Lightfoot pointed out that what Paul said could be paraphrased as, "When I say 'we,' I mean those who are living, those who survive to that day."[1] The Greek does not necessarily mean any more than that. The words speak of those living at the time of Jesus' coming, but they say nothing about whether the speaker would be among them or not. We should bear in mind that Paul has a habit of classing himself with those to whom he is writing at a given time. It is important to notice that he says, "God both raised the Lord and will raise us" (1 Cor 6:14; cf. also 2 Cor 4:14), which classifies him with the dead at the coming of Jesus just as surely as the passage we are looking at places him with the living. We cannot infer from his words anything about whether Paul thought he would live to Christ's coming or not. What he is sure of is that his Lord will come.

Some try to hold these passages in balance by saying that at the time when he wrote the first letter to the Thessalonians Paul thought the coming of the Lord was near. His thought, it is alleged, was far from static. As it developed over the succeeding years, he changed his mind and held that he would die before Christ's return. The dates, however, are against this. Paul's conversion must be dated in the early 30s, and 1 Thessalonians seems to have been written about A.D. 50. The date of 1 Corinthians is not certain, but most scholars put it in the mid 50s (C. K. Barrett thinks early 54 or toward the end of 53[2]). No good reason has been suggested why Paul should have held the view for nearly twenty years that Christ's return was imminent and then abandon it during the next three or four years.

There is no reason for thinking that the Thessalonians did not have a satisfactory understanding of the truth that at the end of this age there will be a general resurrection and that believers who have died before that great day will be raised. Evidently they thought that Jesus would return to earth first, and only after that would the dead rise. Paul assures them that believers still on earth will have no precedence over "those who have fallen asleep." He uses an emphatic negative to make it clear that they will "certainly not" (NIV) have an advantage over their friends.

Events at the coming of Christ

Paul proceeds to enlighten his correspondents about what will happen when Christ comes. He starts by saying, "The Lord himself" will come (1 Thess 4:16), the "himself" making it clear that he is referring to a personal coming, not the sending of a representative. He lists three events that will mark the coming as distinctive: a shout, an archangel's voice, and God's trumpet. Perhaps we should notice that there are those who think that Paul is talking about one loud noise which might be called any one of these. Thus Frame gives the meaning as, "At a command, namely, at an archangel's voice and at a trumpet of God."[3] William Hendriksen finds two loud noises, the "shouted command" and "the archangel . . . sounding God's trumpet."[4] Such views are no doubt possible, but it is much more natural to understand the apostle as meaning that there will be three separate happenings.

J. B. Phillips brings out something of the vigor of the original with his translation: "One word of command, one shout from the Archangel, one blast from the trumpet of God and God in Person will come down from Heaven!" Paul first refers to a "shout," where he makes use of a word that expresses authority. It is used in a variety of ways, such as the shout of an officer to his soldiers, the call of the shipmaster to his rowers, the cry of a hunter to his hounds, or the shout of a charioteer to his horses. The word has about it a note of urgency and authority. Curiously Paul does not say who will utter the shout, but we should probably understand that it is the Lord himself. Elsewhere we read that all who are in the tombs will hear the voice of the Son of God (John 5:28), and it would seem that it is this to which Paul refers.

There will also be the voice of an archangel. People have sometimes tried to identify the archangel, and Michael is usually favored because he is the only archangel named in the New Testament (Jude 9; Gabriel is named in Luke 1, but he is not called an archangel). This is a slender basis for identification. The fact is that since Paul does not name him, we have no way of identifying him. All we can say is that on that great day the Lord's voice will not be the only one to be heard, there will be an archangel who will also utter his voice.

The third phenomenon will be the "trumpet of God." Trumpets are often mentioned in the Old Testament in connection with great religious festivals (Pss 81:3; 150:3). References to a trumpet or a "great trumpet" at times of divine activity are particularly significant (Exod 19:16; Isa 27:13; Joel 2:1; Zech 9:14). It was evidently thought to be a very suitable accompaniment to the great things that God does. In Revelation we read of a voice like the sound of a trumpet (Rev 1:10; 4:1), which is one reason why some think of the trumpet here as another way of referring to a great voice. This is certainly possible, but it seems better to think of

The Last Things

three great sounds. Elsewhere Paul speaks of "the last trumpet" (1 Cor 15:52) and adds the information that when it sounds, "the dead will be raised incorruptible and we shall be changed." He does not add this information here, but then he is not giving a full account of what is to take place on that day. He is dealing with a particular problem that his converts in Thessalonica were facing. Nonetheless, that a trumpet would sound is a thought to which Paul gives expression more than once.

This majestic introduction is followed by the information that the Lord "will come down from heaven" and then "the dead in Christ will be raised first." Their friends had feared that they would miss the great day; instead, Paul tells them, they will have a place of special honor in all that will then be done. It is interesting that the faithful departed are spoken of as "the dead in Christ." With this we should compare "those who have fallen asleep in Christ" (1 Cor 15:18) and "the dead that die in the Lord" (Rev 14:13). Such expressions bring out the truth that Jesus is Lord over death. His people are "in Christ." They are in Christ during the time of this earthly pilgrimage, and they do not cease to be "in Christ" following their deaths. We should perhaps notice that the verb "will be raised" is passive. Paul is not saying that they will rise, as though this were a natural process. He is telling us of something that will be done to the dead believers, something that God will do to them. It is he who will bring them out of the tombs into the life of the world to come.

As we noted earlier, Paul is not giving a full description of all that will happen at the End. Some students of Revelation 20 see here a reference to the first resurrection (Rev 20:5-6), but we should remember that the apostle is not differentiating the resurrection of believers from that of nonbelievers. He is distinguishing between those who die "in Christ" and those who will still be alive when the Lord returns. He is dealing with a subject different from that under discussion in Revelation 20.

The "rapture" of believers

Paul goes on to speak of believers being caught up to meet the Lord, a process popularly called the "rapture" (a term derived from the Latin word for "seize"). It is important to realize that this is the only place in the New Testament that refers unambiguously to this "rapture." There are other places that some readers hold to refer to it, but none make it clear that there will be a rapture of believers. In some quarters there is tremendous emphasis on the rapture, and people have gone into detail as to the way it will all take place. If we are to be biblical, though, we must beware of going beyond what Paul says here, for there is no certainty that a rapture is in mind in any other passage in the New Testament. Anything we may say about it is speculation.

Paul says three great things about the rapture: believers still alive when the Lord comes back will be reunited with believers who have died before them, they will be caught up with an irresistible force, and they will be with the Lord. These are the things that matter. We will look at them in turn.

1. *Reunion.* Paul turns his attention to those believers who survive until that day. He uses the emphatic *"we"* and adds "the living who remain" (1 Thess 4:17). He has made it clear that deceased believers will not be disadvantaged, but he is equally certain that believers who are alive at that time will share in the wonderful happenings. He puts some emphasis on "together with them," partly by placing it early in the sentence (it comes before the verb) and partly by reinforcing the preposition we translate as "with" by prefixing it with another word (which may be an adverb or a preposition), which itself conveys the idea of togetherness or simultaneity.

The result is to emphasize togetherness, to stress the fact that believers, whether they have died prior to or lived through to the great day, will be *together*. The Thessalonians were disturbed at their separation from believers who had died. Paul reassures them by pointing to their oneness in Christ. There will be no separation at the last great day.

2. *"Caught up."* He goes on to say that the living believers will be "caught up in clouds to meet the Lord." The verb is often used of violent action, a "snatching away" of a thing or a person. This may be a disaster as when the evil one snatches away the seed that is sown in someone's heart (Matt 13:19) or when the wolf seizes the sheep (John 10:12). With such usage, it is comforting to know that nothing will snatch believers from the hand of the Son or of the Father (John 10:28, 29). The word is also used of beneficial actions. Thus the Spirit of the Lord caught up Philip (Acts 8:39), and Paul speaks of a man "caught up to the third heaven" or "to Paradise" (2 Cor 12:2, 4). When Paul was in trouble at the hands of the Jerusalem mob the commander ordered his soldiers to snatch him away from them (Acts 23:10).

The verb thus has to do with seizing by force, and Paul is here referring to a force great enough to separate living believers from this earthly life and to reunite them with their departed friends and with their living Lord. The term "rapture" expresses something of the irresistible force that catches believers up, a force that neither they nor any of their opponents can resist.

We will be caught up, Paul says, "in clouds," which accords with the fact that clouds are often associated in Scripture with the presence of God. There were clouds on Mount Sinai when the law was given (Exod 19:16), when the tabernacle was set up (Exod 40:34), and when the temple was brought into use (1 Kgs 8:10–11). We should also remember the cloud at the mount of Jesus' Transfiguration (Mark 9:7) and at his ascension (Acts 1:9). The present passage is in line with those others, and it brings out from another angle the reality of the presence of God.

3. Meeting with the Lord. "To meet the Lord" makes use of an expression that may be used of ordinary meetings, whether friendly or hostile. It is also used of more formal and official meetings. Moulton and Milligan note its use in the papyri: "The word seems to have been a kind of technical term for the official welcome of a newly arrived dignitary—a usage which accords excellently with its NT usage."[5] There are many accounts of emperors or other leaders paying official visits that are described using this term. It is suitable for a great occasion, and Paul uses it this way.

When it is used of official welcomes, people apparently went out to meet the dignitary and then escorted him back to the place where he was going (cf. Matt 25:6; Acts 28:15). This has sometimes been brought into an argument that when believers are caught up to meet the Lord, they form a kind of welcoming party and escort him back to earth. This may indeed be the case, but we should be clear that Paul does not say as much. Indeed it is difficult to see whether he means that when the Lord is united with his people (both the dead and the living), he proceeds to earth or whether he takes them with him back to heaven. Either possibility would accord with the language he uses here. We may be curious about the point, but we should recognize that Paul is not trying to satisfy our curiosity. He is concerned with the wonderful reunion that God will bring about and its permanent consequences.

The meeting, Paul says, will take place "in the air," a truth which in any case follows from our being caught up to a meeting in the clouds. We should also bear in mind the fact that in Paul's time the air was seen as the abode of demons. Satan may be called "the prince of the power of the air" (Eph 2:2). If this is in mind in this passage, then there will be the thought that the returning Lord has defeated the demons; they have been routed in what the ancient world regarded as their own territory. This would then be an expression of the complete defeat, brought about by Christ, of all the forces of evil. "And so we shall be always with the Lord." This is what it all leads up to, and Paul adds no more. Other parts of Scripture tell us of harps and crowns, of streets paved with gold and much more that brings out the wonder and the splendor of it all. Here, however, Paul is making the one important point that to be with the Lord means to enter final bliss. It is his presence (rather than the splendor of his surroundings that is described elsewhere) which is the ultimate blessing. We are reminded of Jesus' own words that to know the Father and Jesus himself "is" (not "brings") "the life eternal" (John 17:3).

Judgment

It is a standard New Testament teaching that when the Lord returns, life as we know it here on earth will cease and there will be a judgment of all, both the living and the dead. This will be the judgment of God (Rom 2:16), but he will bring it about through Christ (Acts 17:31). Thus we read of people standing at the judgment seat of God (Rom 14:10) and elsewhere at the judgment seat of Christ (2 Cor 5:10). In the passages we have looked at in connection with the coming of our Lord thus far, we have seen only that he will come in glory and that he will reunite believers separated by death. Paul, of course, is not unmindful of the sterner aspects of this coming, and elsewhere he devotes some space to bringing out what this means.

Here he writes to the Thessalonians, "if indeed it is a just thing with God to recompense affliction to those who afflict you" (2 Thess 1:6; the clause is introduced with "if," but this throws no doubt on the proposition; it means "if" [as in the case]). Paul has just told his converts that the way they bear up under the opposition of evil is a manifest token of God's righteous judgment (v 5) and they should never forget that God's enabling of his people to endure persecution is part of his "righteous judgment." That does not mean that the persecutors will escape punishment for ever. What Paul is saying here is that in due time evil people will be punished. Justice demands it. Specifically, those who afflict God's people will themselves be afflicted. This is not vengeance; there is nothing vindictive about what Paul is writing. The apostle is simply making it clear that God has made this a moral universe. Evil may go unpunished for a time, but not for ever. This is impossible when we see that God is the God revealed in the Bible.

With this understanding of justice as his point of departure, Paul then links "rest" for the afflicted Thessalonians and, interestingly, "rest with us" (2 Thess 1:7). When we are thinking of the great apostle as bringing consolation and encouragement to his persecuted friends, it is easy to think of him as living in a different atmosphere. We tend to forget that he shared the same world as that inhabited by the Thessalonians; he, too, was afflicted (cf. 2 Cor 11:23–29). At this point he is not dealing with his own sufferings but with those of his friends. It is a little human touch that he remembers that he, too, knows what it is to suffer. The word he uses for "rest" is often used in the sense it has here, namely, rest from afflictions and troubles; that is, relief.

This rest, Paul says, will come about "at the revelation of our Lord Jesus from heaven." He has moved now from what is happening in the daily life of the Thessalonians to what will happen at the end of the age. He does not speak here of the "coming" of the Lord Jesus but of the "revelation" of the Lord. The word speaks of making known something that was not known hitherto. To the world, Jesus was no more than a Galilean peasant. To the Thessalonians who

53   The Last Things

did not respond when the gospel was preached to them, he was simply a Jewish religious teacher, one whom they could easily reject and whose followers they could abuse with impunity. Yet when Jesus comes again, it will be a revelation. They will see him as he is, not as they, in their blindness, had fancied him to be. "At the revelation" is more literally "in the revelation," and this may perhaps signify that the punishment of evil is part of the revelation. We should not think that our Lord is neutral to evil. He is opposed to it totally, and the retribution that will eventually overtake evildoers is part of the revelation of what he is.

Majesty

As he speaks of the coming of the Lord, Paul lets his readers know that this will not be in lowliness like his former coming. He will come "from heaven," which points to his glorious origin, and he will come "with angels of his power," which may well mean "with his powerful angels" as many take it (cf. Ps 103:20). An objection to this way of looking at the expression is that the passage is telling us something about our Lord and that it is his power rather than that of the angels that is in view. The Jerusalem Bible translates the phrase as "the angels of his power," and if we take it this way, the passage is telling us that Jesus will return in power with the angels appropriate to his nature and position.

The second thing we learn about the coming is that it will be "in flaming fire" (2 Thess 1:8). Fire is associated with the divine presence in a number of Old Testament passages (e.g., Exod 19:18; Ps 18:8), so it is a very suitable accompaniment of the returning Lord. It is all the more appropriate in that the passage goes on to speak of his "giving retribution" to sinners. We are reminded of some words in Isaiah: "For behold, the Lord will come in fire, and his chariots like the storm-wind, to render his anger in fury, and his rebuke with flames of fire. For by fire will the Lord execute judgment" (Isa 66:15–16). Like the Lord in the Old Testament, the Lord Jesus at his coming will provide the retribution that is fittingly described in terms of fire.

The sinners singled out are "those who do not know God and those who do not obey the gospel of our Lord Jesus." Paul is not referring to people who have never had the opportunity of knowing God but rather to people who "did not approve to have God in knowledge" (Rom 1:28). There are those who respond to the revelation God has given them and those who reject it. Paul is saying that those who reject the light God has given are guilty people and, in the end, they will be confronted with that judgment described in terms of flaming fire.

Their refusal to know God is the result of deliberate choice, and this comes out in the fact that they are described also as "those who do not obey the gospel of our Lord Jesus." It is true that the definite article is repeated before the second expression, and it is possible to take this to mean that a new group of people is in mind. Some who understand the passage this way think that the former expression means Gentile sinners and the latter Jewish sinners. If such a distinction were in mind, it would surely not be expressed so obscurely that the reader has to make an inference to find it. The language in which the suggested distinction is made is far from definite and certainly insufficient to carry conviction. In any case, the whole passage is written in the style of the oracles of the Old Testament, where expressions like those we are considering would naturally be understood as forming an example of synonymous parallelism. In other words, "those who do not know God" and "those who do not obey the gospel of our Lord Jesus" are two ways of describing the same people. They had been offered the same salvation as the Thessalonian Christians they were persecuting, but they had refused it. Their refusal to obey the gospel was culpable. At the coming

The Last Things

of that same Lord Jesus whose gospel they had refused, they would pay the penalty of their refusal.

This is explicitly spelled out by Paul. These sinners "will pay the penalty, eternal destruction from the face of the Lord and from the glory of his might." The word translated "penalty" is related to words like "just" and "retribution" in the previous verses. In other words, the apostle is continuing the thought of justice; he is not talking about an arbitrary punishment but the working out of what is right. These sinners will receive the just consequence of what they have done.

We should not understand "destruction" as annihilation. Rather we should remember that the word may have the meaning "ruin" (RSV translates it this way in 1 Tim 6:9). In the present passage it is surely the opposite of "eternal life," the life of the world to come. Eternal life is, of course, endless, but more important than this is the fact that it is a life of a particular quality, a life in fellowship with God. The ruin of which Paul speaks here, he says, is "from" the face of the Lord, which we should understand in the sense "away from" the face of the Lord. Just as eternal life is life in the presence of the Lord, so eternal ruin is separation from the presence of the Lord (cf. Matt 25:41, 46).

Paul speaks of a grim reality. He makes it clear that those who preach the gospel are not idly playing a game in which it does not matter who wins and who loses. They hold out eternal life and eternal ruin. The refusal of a careless generation to face up to the only two possibilities ultimately open to them does not alter the reality. Those who reject the gospel will in the end exclude themselves from the presence of the Lord. "Face," of course, in this expression stands for the whole person. Those who refuse remove themselves from the divine presence.

The foolishness of this refusal is brought out by the addition of "and from the glory of his might." Jesus had been a lowly person here on earth, and his messengers had had nothing wonderful about them when they went to Thessalonica. Yet it is a mistake to take either of these considerations as pointing to ultimate reality. When the Lord Jesus returns to this earth it will be in splendor, and those who have rejected him and his messengers will find that they have rejected more than a peasant from Galilee and some penurious preachers. They have rejected a Lord who is both glorious and powerful. In the end, neither his glory nor his might will be hidden.

Paul speaks of the day "when he comes to be glorified in his holy ones" (2 Thess 1:10). We should not think that the purpose of Christ's coming is concentrated on the punishment of the wicked. That punishment has occupied us in the verses we have looked at, but attention has been fastened on it only because it was a topic of some importance for the Thessalonian Christians in their difficult situation. There is a much more positive aspect to the coming, and it is this to which Paul now turns. It is the glory that is the most significant aspect of the Second Coming, not the ruin of those who refused the glory.

We should probably take "his holy ones" in this passage in the sense "his saints"; that is, those who have accepted the gospel and have been numbered among his followers. The expression is quite general, and it is wide enough to include any who belong to the Lord, whether their origin is in heaven or on earth. So it is theoretically possible to see here a reference to the angels as well as to the redeemed, but there does not seem to be any reason for thinking that Paul has angels in mind. It is much more likely that the "holy ones" are identical with "all them that have believed" later in the verse.

The returning Lord then will be glorified in his saints. This is an unusual expression (and in this precise form is found only in this passage in the New Testament). There has been a good deal of discussion about its precise meaning, but the most likely possibility is that what the Lord has done in

57   *The Last Things*

those who have put their trust in him will then be seen to be truly glorious. On another occasion Paul referred to the time when he had become a Christian and people who had known of his persecuting activities heard what had happened. "And they glorified God in me," he says (Gal 1:24). It is perhaps something like that which is in mind here. It is what the Lord has done in those who are his own that will be seen to be glorious.

Another unusual expression is joined to this, "and to be marveled at in all those who have believed" ("to be marveled at" does not occur anywhere else in the New Testament). The thought is not very dissimilar to that in the earlier part of the verse. What Christ has done in believers is something glorious; it is also something at which those who see it may well marvel. How could the Lord take sinners like Paul and those Thessalonians and make "saints" out of them? Paul may not know how he did it, but he knows that he did do it. He now says that the miracle of grace will be such as to cause astonishment when it is fully known at the last great day. We should not concern ourselves with the question, "Who is it who will marvel on that day?" It may be the angels, or those who have rejected the gospel, or the transformed sinners themselves. Paul gives no attention to that question. He is concerned only with the wonderful thing that happens in those who believe, a wonderful change that takes place right away and which the Lord will sustain until the end of time and beyond.

These then are the passages in which Paul gives sustained treatment to the manner of the Lord's return to earth and what it will mean. We should not overlook the fact that there are other occasions when he refers to the coming, although without sustained treatment, and these occasions should not be overlooked.

Perhaps we might start by noticing that the word "coming,"

parousia, can apply to comings of various kinds. Paul uses it for example of the "comings" of some of his helpers. He writes to the Corinthians of the *parousia* of Stephanas, Fortunatus, and Achaicus (1 Cor 16:17), and in another place he refers to that of Titus (2 Cor 7:6). There are other such uses of the term in the New Testament. There is even a reference to the *parousia* of the Man of Lawlessness (2 Thess 2:9). Characteristically, however, it is used of the Second Coming. It does not have to be described in any way: "the coming," used without qualification, is the coming of Jesus, the *parousia*.

Thus Paul asks his friends, "What is our hope or joy or crown of rejoicing—are not you?—before our Lord Jesus at his coming?" (1 Thess 2:19). The apostle makes it clear that he held his converts in the highest esteem. He has not been able to visit them, but that did not mean that he had forgotten them or that they had fallen in his estimation. He brings this out by telling them what they will mean to him on that last great day. If they will mean so much to him at a time when all the attention will be elsewhere, namely, on the majesty of the Lord, then it is impossible to exaggerate his concern for them here and now.

Other passages drive home the importance of Christian qualities by relating them to the Lord's *parousia*. We see this in the prayer that God the Father and our Lord Jesus will make the converts abound in love "so that he may establish your hearts blameless in holiness before our God and Father at the *parousia* of our Lord Jesus with all his holy ones" (1 Thess 3:13). It is important that believers live uprightly, and it is not uncommon for Paul to emphasize the importance of love. For him it is only in love that people will be blameless in heart, and his prayer accordingly is for this to happen in his Thessalonian converts. His reference to "holiness" is not to be overlooked. "Blameless" might be understood as signifying outstanding ethical achievement, but "holiness" is a religious term; it points to the state of the preachers before God.

We should bear in mind that Paul's word for "holiness" is an unusual one. In the Greek translation of the Old Testament it is never used of people but always refers to God. Elsewhere in the New Testament it refers to the Holy Spirit or to Christ (Rom 1:4) and is part of an exhortation to "perfecting holiness" (2 Cor 7:1). So when Paul uses the term here, he is not making a matter-of-fact remark about something quite ordinary. He is setting the highest possible standard before the Thessalonians and praying that God will bring it to pass and that he will bring it to pass not only here and now but in such a way that it persists into the day when Christ comes back. It is an extraordinary concept that believers will have this kind of holy blamelessness before God and the denizens of heaven.

The thought of blamelessness at the *parousia* of the Lord Jesus surfaces again toward the end of the first letter when Paul prays for it once more. He asks that the Thessalonians may be sanctified completely and that their "spirit and soul and body be kept entire, blameless at the coming of our Lord Jesus Christ" (1 Thess 5:23). Again blamelessness is linked with sanctification; the two go together in a way that should lead us to think of both a religious and an ethical aspect to the life of the believer. There is also the thought of completion. Paul uses an unusual word (the only occurrence in the New Testament) for "completely"; it brings to expression the thought that nothing should be lacking in the sanctification for which he prays.

He goes on to bring this out by specifying the "spirit and soul and body" of the Thessalonians. We should probably not understand this as an affirmation that we are made up of three parts, over against those who hold that there are only two parts (body and soul). There is no reason for thinking that Paul has in mind a strict classification of the various segments that go to make up a human being. He is simply using an ordinary way of speaking to bring out his point that he looks for every part of the Thessalonians to be affected by the sanctification for which he prays.

The apostle has another unusual word (found elsewhere in the New Testament only in Jas 1:4) when he looks for the believers to be kept "entire." A standard lexicon says of it: "a qualitative term, *with integrity, whole, complete, undamaged, intact, blameless.*"[6] The word indicates that the people in question should be complete, sound, entire. Clearly Paul is stretching his vocabulary at this point to bring out the truth that he is looking for the Thessalonian Christians to live on the highest plane. That they should fulfill all that he looks for in this passage means that they would have an extraordinary standard indeed. He prays that they will have it and that it should be manifest at Christ's *parousia.* Once again the coming of the Lord is brought into a prayer for the utmost in sanctification and ethical achievement.

In one instance Paul brings the *parousia* into a request for the Thessalonians to act: "Now we ask you, brothers," he says, "with respect to the coming of our Lord Jesus Christ and our being gathered to him that you be not quickly moved" (2 Thess 2:1). The word translated here "with respect to" often has the meaning "on behalf of," and it may have something of the flavor of "in the interest of the truth concerning." It is not the word we would have expected in this place. The main thing that Paul is doing is directing the attention of his converts to the *parousia* and urging them to live lives appropriate to the fact that one day they will be caught up to be with the Lord for ever. That the coming of the Lord should be a strong stimulus to right Christian behavior comes out in the prayers that we have noticed. Here we see much the same thing, but this time it comes in the form of an exhortation: "Seeing that one day we will be with the Lord, what manner of people ought we to be?"

In our next chapter we will be looking at the manifestation of the Man of Lawlessness in the last days. We will see then that he is the epitome of all that is evil. As Paul writes about this evil figure, he brings him into connection with our Lord's *parousia*. He says that the Lord Jesus "will destroy him with the breath of his mouth and bring him to nothing with the manifestation of his coming" (2 Thess 2:8). The apostle is making it clear that Christ will be far too powerful for the evil one and will not need to put forward all his might; "the breath of his mouth" will be sufficient (cf. Luther's hymn, "A word shall quickly slay him").

He is also saying that the *parousia* itself will bring about the undoing of the Man of Lawlessness. Up to now we have thought of the *parousia* as a wonderful and glorious happening that will bring comfort and strength to God's persecuted saints. It will deliver them from the trials and problems of this mortal life and from the weakness that accompanies his people in all they do. We are told in this passage that that is not all. The coming of the Lord in itself will bring evil down. The verb Paul uses is difficult to translate. It occurs twenty-seven times in the New Testament, and the King James Version rendered it seventeen different ways. The Revised Version reduced those variations to ten but introduced three additional translations. Every translation has increased the number, and more than eighty renderings have been used. Thus, it is no small wonder that it is difficult to find a single (and simple) English equivalent. Basically the word has a meaning like "render inoperative," "make null and void," and this helps us to see what is in mind here. The coming of Jesus in itself means the end of the power of evil. No matter how strong evil appears to weaker mortals, it cannot stand in the presence of the triumphant Lord.

4   THE DEFEAT OF EVIL

Christians have always been opposed by evil forces, and they can never have felt that life is easy. Paul is certain that it will always be like this, but he makes it plain that the worst of the evil forces will be encountered only at the end of this world. At that time there will be an outbreak of evil headed by one whom he calls the "Man of Lawlessness," a title which occurs in the New Testament only in 2 Thessalonians 2.

The title "Man of Lawlessness" tells us something significant about this being: he is not subject to law. Paul links him with "the rebellion" (2 Thess 2:3), a word which may mean religious or political rebellion and here seems to include both. He is saying that at the end of this age there will be a great uprising of the forces of evil in rebellion against God and that this rebellion will be led by a being who has no regard for law. This being is also called "the son of perdition," that is, his character will be "lostness."

He will claim for himself the place of highest authority and, not content with supreme political power, he will take his seat "in the sanctuary of God" (2 Thess 2:4), an expression that has been understood several ways. The word "sanctuary" is sometimes used metaphorically of the Christian church (Eph 2:21) or of the body of the Christian (1 Cor 6:19), from which some have deduced that the Man of Lawlessness will take over the Christian church and make it his base. Against this is the fact that, while the New Testament envisages that many will fall away in the last days, it does not teach that the whole church will become apostate. In any case the word "sanctuary" mostly means a material building. It is used properly of the innermost shrine (just as the word "temple" includes the whole complex, with vestries, courtyards, and the like); "sanctuary" is the place where deity is especially thought to dwell. Attempts have been made to identify this shrine, but Paul gives us no clue to its whereabouts. He is not telling his readers where all this will happen but, instead, what it means.

When the Man of Lawlessness takes his seat in the sanctuary he is making a claim to the highest place of all, the place of God. Clearly Paul expects that in the end time wickedness will be present on a scale greater than anything previously known and that there will be a leader who will claim for himself the place that belongs only to God.

In a very puzzling expression Paul says that the Thessalonians know "what is restraining" this Man of Lawlessness, and goes on to refer to "the mystery of lawlessness" that is already at work, and further to "him who restrains" who will in due course be taken out of the way (2 Thess 2:6–7). There is a problem in identifying the restrainer, which is spoken of both as neuter ("what is restraining") and as masculine ("him who restrains"). Some identify the restrainer as the Roman Empire, which might be thought of in itself or in the person of its emperor. If this was Paul's view, he was in error because the Roman Empire has passed away and the Man of Lawlessness has not yet made his appearance. Oscar Cullmann saw "a reference to the missionary preaching as a sign pointing to the end,"[1] while Paul, he thought, was the personal restrainer. Not many have accepted this view; nothing in the letter gives the impression that Paul saw himself as holding back the coming of the Man of Lawlessness.

Other suggestions include the Jewish state (but how could that state hold back the eschatological forces of evil?) or God the Father or the Holy Spirit (but how can either be taken out of the way?). There seems little point in running through the conjectures. Probably the best suggestion is that Paul has in mind the rule of law as it is manifested in ordered government. In his day it was evident in the Roman Empire and since then it has been manifested in a variety of states. It accords with the "Man of Lawlessness" that his time of triumph is seen in the doing away with law. As we noted earlier, his very title points to his being the antithesis of law; he is opposed to law and to all the institutions that uphold law.

Paul speaks of the *parousia* of this being: he will have a "coming" that can be described with the same word as that used so often of the coming of Christ. Paul goes on to link this coming with "the working of Satan," which he goes on to describe in several ways (2 Thess 2:9-10). It adds up to the thought that there will be a tremendous upsurge of evil in the last days and that Satan will be active through his minions.

It is perhaps not unnatural that Christians have spent a lot of time trying to determine just who the Man of Lawlessness is and precisely what restrains him. Questions like this seem to have a perennial attraction for some believers. Paul's interest, however, is not in such questions; his interest is rather in the total overthrow of the powers of evil. He says that the Lawless One will be revealed and immediately goes on, "whom the Lord Jesus will destroy with the breath of his mouth and bring to nothing by the manifestation of his coming" (2 Thess 2:8). No action is necessary; the very appearance of the Lord Jesus will destroy the might of the

65   *The Defeat of Evil*

evil one. Paul speaks of the misdeeds of the followers of the Man of Lawlessness and goes on to say that God is at work in sending the delusion they hold so firmly (even in the "working of error," whereby they "believe the lie" [2 Thess 2:11], a purpose of God is fulfilled). All those who reject the truth will be judged (2 Thess 2:12).

Persecution

In addition to the passage in which he speaks of the climactic opposition of evil to God at the end time, Paul has a number of references to the evil that people do here and now. So important is this to Ronald Ward that he begins his study of the theology of the Thessalonian epistles with their teaching on sin.[2] We should not think that Paul has a morbid interest in the way evil so easily flourishes in this imperfect world. Rather he is certain that evil will not triumph in the end. He is sure of the existence of God and the power of God, and he is sure that in Christ God has taken decisive action to defeat evil and to make it possible for sinners to receive forgiveness and to enter into newness of life, a life in which sin is not dominant.

Paul has a variety of ways of underlining the truth that Christ has defeated evil and that Christ's people may well take heart, no matter how difficult their circumstances. One feature of the Thessalonian correspondence is the way the apostle brings out the fact of the triumph of good and the certainty that, in the end, it will defeat every force of evil.

Consider Paul's treatment of persecution. He speaks of the persecutions already inflicted on God's people and shows that these actions of evil people had not defeated the purposes of God. Clearly this was something that mattered a good deal to him and to the Thessalonians. The new converts had themselves undergone suffering, and Paul could speak of "all your persecutions and the afflictions you endure." These he sees as a demonstration of God's righteous judgment, so that they should be deemed worthy of "the kingdom of God, for which you also suffer" (2 Thess 1:4-5). Now no one in the New Testament believes that there is any possibility that the kingdom of God will be overthrown. Suffering for the kingdom is thus not in vain; suffering itself points to ultimate victory.

Paul also refers specifically to the persecution undergone by the churches of God in Judea, a persecution like the one the Thessalonians had endured (1 Thess 2:14). Neither had stamped out the people of God, and in both cases there had been triumph as well as suffering.

Persecution entails more than the sufferings of believers, however, and Paul goes on to particularize his argument with the killing of Jesus and the prophets and the persecution of the Christian preachers. These were certainly evil actions and no doubt it seemed to the persecutors, and possibly to bystanders who observed what was going on, that those who opposed the purposes of God in such ways had accomplished a great deal.

Wrath

Paul viewed such perceptions as superficial understanding. He ends the passage on the Judean persecutions by saying, "the wrath has come upon them to the end" (or "to the uttermost"; 1 Thess 2:16). Some translations read "retribution" (e.g., NEB), but this is not the meaning of the Greek; the word means "wrath." There is no question that this "wrath" is God's wrath. Paul is surely referring to a preliminary manifestation of the eschatological wrath, and he sees it as certain that the persecutors will receive it to the full. Some commentators find it hard to see these words as genuinely Paul's; they find a much softer attitude toward the Jews in Romans 9-11.

We should remember that in Romans Paul is writing about God's purposes for Israel, not about the fate of those Jews who persecute the people of God. Here in Thessalonians he is not concerned with the ultimate destiny of the nation but rather with the truth that the persecutors will not succeed in destroying God's church. They will only store up wrath for themselves.

Paul has some other references to the divine wrath, and they press home the point that believers need not fear that wrath. The apostle reminds the Thessalonians that they are awaiting God's Son from heaven, "Jesus, who delivers us from the coming wrath" (1 Thess 1:10). The present participle is timeless, with a meaning like "the deliverer." It does not mean that Paul is talking in terms of a "realized" eschatology. This is made clear by the fact that he speaks of the wrath specifically as "the coming wrath"; he is referring to the end of the age. He is saying that when people put their trust in Jesus they are safe, safe now and safe at the end of the age when the divine wrath will be brought to bear on sinners who will receive the due reward of their deeds. For our purpose, the significant theme is the deliverance of believers, not the punishment of sinners. Paul sees evil as overcome in the lives of believers and overcome in such a way that they are secure eternally.

This truth is brought out in another way when the apostle writes, "God has not appointed us for wrath but for the obtaining of salvation through our Lord Jesus Christ" (1 Thess 5:9). Here we have both the negative and the positive aspects of salvation: we do not experience God's wrath, but we do experience our Lord Jesus Christ's salvation. Paul looks right through time to God's setting up of the final state of affairs, and there he finds believers delivered from the wrath. Wrath is not God's purpose for them—salvation is. Once again we see that evil is conquered.

We sometimes get much the same idea without the word "wrath." Thus Paul refers to "those who perish, because they did not receive the love of the truth in order that they might be saved" (2 Thess 2:10). The fact that these sinners perish shows the seriousness of God's opposition to all that is evil. With that, however, we notice "the love of the truth" that leads to salvation. Once again there is the thought that God and good are powerful and that there is an ultimate triumph over evil for all those who put their trust in God.

Suffering

From another point of view the troubles of the converts were those that Paul had predicted (1 Thess 3:4). They were not outside the control of God. Indeed, Paul says that we Christians "are appointed" to sufferings (v 3). This is an important part of the apostle's understanding of trouble and of life. It may connect with the persecutions we were looking at earlier, for persecutions certainly mean trouble. The cause of evil, however, may prosper when troubles of other kinds put believers in difficulties. Paul assures his readers that this kind of evil cannot defeat God's purposes in his people.

Believers must not expect an easy path through life. They are appointed to suffer, and in some way they certainly will suffer. They are not to complain bitterly when suffering comes as though some strange and unexpected disaster had struck them. In a world as evil as the one Paul lived in (and as the one Christians have lived in ever since) suffering is inevitable. Yet Paul is saying something more than that. He is saying that suffering is part of God's purpose for us. We may not understand why this should be so, but at least we can reflect that suffering produces qualities of character in those who endure it rightly, qualities of character that do not make their appearance in the times of peace and ease. To understand that God has appointed us to suffering puts meaning into life when dark and difficult days come.

Indeed, suffering does not necessarily mean misery and unhappiness. Taken in the right way, and recognized as God's meaningful discipline, it may mean the reverse. Paul says that when the Thessalonians "received the word," they did so "in great affliction with joy of the Holy Spirit" (1 Thess 1:6). Becoming Christians had exposed them to hardships in a city that did not approve of what they were doing and was ready to ridicule and oppose them. They did not hold on to their newfound faith solely by a spirit of grim determination. Like many believers in the centuries that followed, they found exhilaration in the midst of their troubles. The Holy Spirit himself was in their hearts, and this meant joy. It meant a joy that the world did not give and which the world could never take away.

Paul appeals to his own experience when he says that he and his companions were entrusted with the gospel that they preach, "not as pleasing men, but God who tests our hearts" (1 Thess 2:4). He does not say in what way God conducts these tests, but it is clear that the heavenly Father searches people's innermost beings. In the fact that God then approves some to be his preachers, we see from quite a different angle that there are people in whom evil has been defeated.

The Thessalonians had known what Paul predicted: he had made himself quite clear (1 Thess 3:4; W. G. Rutherford tries to bring out the significance of the continuous tense with "the warning was often on our lips"). Persecution would thus not have taken them by surprise. Although he had predicted that persecution would come, Paul was not sure how these infant believers would behave under stress, and he sent Timothy to strengthen them (1 Thess 3:2). We see something of his delight when Timothy reported that they were standing up so well (1 Thess 3:6-10). In their own experience they had come to know something of the triumph of God over such evils as persecution.

This had been a matter of legitimate pride for Paul and his colleagues. They boasted in the other churches about the way the Thessalonians had borne their persecutions. Another thought was linked to this spirit of endurance, which we earlier discussed, in that they saw it as no less than justice that God would in due course recompense the persecutors (2 Thess 1:4–7). Paul is clear that evil people will not escape indefinitely. Sooner or later their evil deeds will receive their due recompense in the providence of God.

It is in line with all this that Paul recommends prayer, that the believers should be delivered from unreasonable and evil men (2 Thess 3:2). They should not rely on their own strength in the face of such strong enemies as those that confronted them, but neither should they be dismayed. God is stronger than evil and will in the end decisively eliminate it. In the meantime, believers should use the weapon of prayer and know that God will surely answer them and not suffer evil people to prevail over them.

In matters like these Paul is no ivory-tower theorist. He knew what it was to suffer in the service of Christ (2 Cor 11:23–28). So now he speaks of his own sufferings and his endurance of insults in the time before he came to Thessalonica (1 Thess 2:2). These things did not mean that the progress of the gospel was prevented. These hardships simply meant that Paul went on to city after city founding new churches and bringing other people into God's salvation. God is not defeated by the opposition evil people throw up before his messengers.

Satan

Sometimes Paul refers to the activity of the evil one, but when he does he is mindful that God is greater. That does not mean that Satan should be disregarded as completely ineffective. The evil one is active and constantly opposes and harasses believers in their service of God. For example, the apostle tells his correspondents that the preachers, and specifically he himself, had wanted to come back to Thessalonica, but Satan had hindered them (1 Thess 2:18). We need not doubt that God overruled these plans in the sense that he had other work for Paul to do at that time, but the incidental glimpse of the power allowed to the evil one is of interest. He does hinder the servants of God and sometimes stops them from doing work they would very much like to do and which they see as setting forward the cause of right. All that he does, however, is within the overarching purpose of God: he can do nothing that God does not permit him to do. That means that if he stops one of God's servants from accomplishing some service of God, then that servant may be assured that God is in charge of the whole process. In ways we expect or not, the good purpose of God is set forward. There are mysteries, but in the end Satan cannot defeat the divine purpose.

In another place we read that Paul had made an inquiry about the faith of the Thessalonian converts, "lest the tempter had tempted you and our work had been in vain" (1 Thess 3:5). Had they fallen away, the work of the apostles would have been "in vain," but God did not allow that. The power of evil is not sufficient to overthrow the plan of God. Paul's implication is that his inquiry had shown that the tempter had been unsuccessful: the work that the preachers had done continued to develop.

This is also the implication of the apostle's exhortation, "But *you*, brothers, do not be weary in doing good" (2 Thess 3:13). There is an emphatic *"you"* that sets the believers apart from the offenders mentioned in the previous verses. Brothers in the faith (i.e., Paul's fellow believers) may be exhorted to continue with their good works; for them it is good, not evil, that finally triumphs.

In the end, people cannot get away with sin, and Paul reminds his readers that God punishes evil (1 Thess 4:6). Satan is not specifically mentioned at this point, but there is a clear implication that in the end the evil one will not be strong enough to preserve those who follow his ways. When they are confronted by God, the limitations of the power of evil will be manifest. God will certainly punish wickedness, and there is nothing Satan can do to stop it.

Believers are constantly being tempted, and, although Paul does not always refer to Satan in this connection, he is sure that believers ought to be warned against accepting low standards, and he is sure that the triumph of God will be manifest in them. Thus they are not to engage in "the passion of lust," like the Gentiles who do not know God (1 Thess 4:5); nor are they to live in uncleanness but rather in sanctification (v 7). From the way he writes, Paul clearly expects that the Thessalonian believers will live sanctified lives.

This is apparent also from a contemplation of their essential nature. Now that they belong to Christ, they belong to the light and to the day, not to the night and to the darkness (1 Thess 5:5). Their conduct will manifest this truth. They are not to engage in the worldly practice of returning evil for evil but always to do good "to one another and to all" (1 Thess 5:15). Clearly Paul expects their good to triumph in such circumstances.

He also expects them to succeed when he says that they are to abstain from every kind of evil (1 Thess 5:22). This expression is sometimes understood in the sense "Abstain from all appearance of evil" (KJV), but while the word rendered "appearance" does indeed sometimes have this meaning, it is never the outward appearance that does not correspond to the inward. It is more likely that the expression here means "every kind of evil," but if it be taken as in the KJV, the meaning would be "every evil that can be seen." Paul writes about evil that is real, not illusory, and he looks for the Thessalonians to overcome evil of every kind in the strength of God.

The Idlers

Paul exhorts the Thessalonians to work with their hands and earn their living (1 Thess 4:11-12). In this way they will both act in a suitable manner toward outsiders and provide for their own living. He has a series of references to people who were "disorderly" (1 Thess 5:14; 2 Thess 3:6-13), and what he says about them shows that their failure to keep to the proper order took the form of a refusal to work for their living. The increased attention he gives the problem in the second letter shows that what he said in the first had not been heeded sufficiently. Paul sees this as bad for the disorderly persons themselves and bad for the reputation of the church to which they belonged. This appears to have been a special problem for the Thessalonian church, because we do not hear of it elsewhere in the New Testament.

Many scholars believe that these people did not work for their living because they expected Christ's return at any moment. What was the point of working at a job when the Lord was about to appear and this whole world system be done away? On the whole it seems that this is the most plausible suggestion, but other views are held. It may be that some of the converts saw themselves as "spiritually minded" people who should give all their time to "spiritual" pursuits and allow their fellow believers the privilege of providing for their daily needs. Or perhaps they saw manual labor as demeaning and thought that those who had been made free by Christ, who were now the children of God, could not be expected to work in the way slaves work. Or they may have seen some form of "quietness" as the essence of the Christian way (some scholars find this in certain forms of Gnosticism and think this was the case in Thessalonica, but Gnosticism has not been shown to have affected this church).

Whatever the cause, Paul sees the practice as deplorable and strongly urges his friends to see that it should be abandoned. The way in which he writes his instructions shows that he is confident that the Thessalonians will handle the problem.

In such passages Paul is simply exhorting his converts to abstain from evil and to do the right. He is obviously confident that they will succeed, at least in the main. He is not writing about a lost cause but about a victory over evil that he expects to be realized in the Thessalonian believers, just as there is to be a victory over evil that will be realized at the end of this age when the Man of Lawlessness will be finally overthrown. There is also a victory that is won day by day by humble followers of Jesus who resist the temptations they constantly encounter and, in the strength of their Lord, experience their own triumphs here and now.

5 THE CHRISTIAN FAMILY

In the New Testament the word "brother" is found 343 times. A few times the word refers to physical brothers, but far and away the most frequent use of the expression in the New Testament is for those who share membership in the heavenly family, those who are children of the one heavenly Father. The Jews had the habit of referring to fellow Jews as brothers, and the early Christians, who, of course, were Jews, sometimes used the term in the same way (cf. Acts 7:2 and quotations from the Old Testament in Acts 3:22; Heb 2:12). In those early days Jewish Christians were called "brother" by other Jews (Acts 2:37; 13:15), and Christian Jews called other Jews by the same name (Acts 7:2; 28:17). Such passages probably tell us how the Christian usage originated, but they are not the usual way Christians employed the term.

Jesus gave the word a new meaning when he said, "Whoever does the will of my Father who is in heaven is my brother and sister and mother" (Matt 12:50). Jesus also discouraged the use of the title "Rabbi" for "one is your teacher and you are all brothers" (Matt 23:8). "Brothers" are those who have experienced the new birth that makes them members of one heavenly family and children of one heavenly Father.

Thus the term comes to be used for fellow Christians, a use that occurs again and again throughout the New Testament. It is fascinating that, in a society where slaves were so little esteemed, the Christian church viewed slaves and their owners as brothers in the Lord. It is not without interest that "brotherhood" is not a common term in the New Testament (it occurs only twice). The Christians were not so much interested in the abstract idea of brotherhood as in the fact that other Christians were their brothers and sisters in the Lord. The word "brother" is found in all parts of the New Testament, but it is especially frequent in Paul (133 times). It occurs with surprising frequency in the short Thessalonian letters (19 times in the first letter and 9 times in the second letter). It is a mark of the warmth of the bond that Paul found between himself and these correspondents.

The apostle speaks of the Thessalonians as "brothers beloved by God" (1 Thess 1:4)[1] and again as "brothers beloved by the Lord" (2 Thess 2:13). There is probably not much difference between the two, for those who are beloved of God the Father are also beloved of God the Son. Both expressions point to the fundamental thing about the Christian brotherhood: the love of God. Christians are not brothers because they are bound together by some natural attraction; they are children of God together because they share in the salvation the love of God has brought about.

Not surprisingly this means that they are bound to one another with strong bonds of affection. Paul says that he and his fellow preachers had been "affectionately desiring" the Thessalonians, where he employs an unusual word which, it has been conjectured, was a term of endearment taken from the nursery. Whether this is so or not, there is no doubt that the word expresses a very warm affection. The apostle goes on that they had been ready to impart to the Thessalonians "not only the gospel of God but also our own souls, because you had become very dear (or, beloved) to us" (1 Thess 2:8). There can be no doubt that Paul felt he was united to the Thessalonian believers by a very strong bond of affection.

Brothers share knowledge

Brotherhood may be linked with common knowledge. Paul writes "you know, brothers, our coming in to you, that it was not in vain" (1 Thess 2:1). The apostle thus appeals to their common knowledge of what had happened during his evangelistic campaign in their city. In the same spirit he speaks of his conviction that they remember his "toil" and "labor" as he and his friends labored so that they should not be a burden to the Thessalonians (1 Thess 2:9). There are things he must tell his fellow believers, but by way of reminder: "Now about the times and the seasons, brothers," he writes, "you have no need that I should write to you" (1 Thess 5:1). Even though there was "no need," he does say a little about them nevertheless; he was a kind brother and did what he could to meet the needs of others in the family. He made sure that the believers would not be lacking in the knowledge that was important in the family. Similarly Paul uses "brothers" as his form of address when he is saying "we do not want you to be ignorant" (1 Thess 4:13). On this occasion he is conveying new information to them, but brotherhood is again a matter of shared knowledge.

It fits in with his idea of brotherhood that he insists that his letter be read to "all" the brothers (1 Thess 5:27). There may have been some special reason for this strong emphasis: his words mean "I adjure you by the Lord that the letter be read to all the brothers." This is a most unusual way of referring to the reading of a letter, and it would have left the

Thessalonians with no doubt that it was important for all to hear it.

Some have felt that the church was divided into two sections, Jewish and Gentile, and that this was a way of ensuring that everybody came to know what Paul had written. Such a division goes against everything we know about the early church, and it is quite unthinkable that Paul would have acquiesced in such a division.

It is not much better with the suggestion that Paul wants the letter read to church leaders as well as the rank and file. Surely when the letter first came to the church the church leaders would be the first to know about it and to hear what was in it. It would be the leaders who would have the responsibility of ensuring that the rank and file came to know what Paul had written, not the rank and file who would have to ensure that the leaders came to hear it.

It is better to think that the expression arises from Paul's strong affection for his Thessalonian converts. He had not been able to visit them, but when they heard this letter they would know that that was not his fault. It was thus important that they should all come to know what he had written. A further suggestion is that there were some, for example, the idlers, who might well not want to hear what Paul wrote, and he insists that they be made to hear. There may be something in this, but Paul's affectionate desire that all the brothers know his attitude seems a better explanation.

Requests and instruction

Quite often Paul appeals to the fact of brotherhood when he is making some request of his correspondents. "We ask you, brothers," he writes, "to know those who labor among you and are over you in the Lord and admonish you" (1 Thess 5:12), and he goes on to urge them to esteem their leaders highly in love for their work's sake. Similarly it is to "the brothers" that he makes request that they "admonish the disorderly, comfort the fainthearted, support the weak, be longsuffering toward all" (1 Thess 5:14). This is a revealing statement of what brotherhood involves; brothers and sisters in the heavenly family have a constant care for each other. They should also look up to their leaders (to see that their admonishments are heeded) and look out for each other (to do what they can to build up the life of the community, whether by way of admonishment or encouragement).

It is in line with this that Paul asks the believers at Thessalonica to pray for him (1 Thess 5:25; 2 Thess 3:1). It is also in line with what brotherhood means that he asks them to stand fast and retain their hold on the traditions (2 Thess 2:15). He similarly commands, "in the name of our Lord Jesus Christ that you keep away from every brother who walks in a disorderly manner and not in accordance with the tradition you received from us" (2 Thess 3:6). Paul also exhorts them not to grow weary in doing well (2 Thess 3:13).

Interestingly he calls on the Thessalonian Christians in their capacity as brothers and sisters to take disciplinary action against offenders; they are to note these persons and not have fellowship with them. "But do not count him as an enemy," Paul says, "but rather admonish him as a brother" (2 Thess 3:15). Being a brother in the full sense is not all sweetness and light. Times will arise when it is necessary to take stern action against a fellow believer who is coming short of the standard he should attain. This is part of being a brother as Paul understands it, and he calls on his readers to do their duty.

Interdependence of the brothers

We are not to think of all the brotherly help that came to the Thessalonians as flowing from Paul and his associates to the new church. Thus we read that the Thessalonians

The Christian Family

became imitators of the churches of Judea. Unfortunately that imitation was due to the persecutions they, like the Judean believers, had undergone (1 Thess 2:14). It matters a great deal that they had profited from the examples of those earlier believers. Christians can be of help to other Christians by their demonstration that the grace of God will always see them through their troubles.

There is a somewhat different thought in Paul's lament that he and his associates had been "orphaned" from the Thessalonians (1 Thess 2:17). His sense of fellowship and brotherhood was such that when he was not able to be with his friends as he wished he felt like an orphan. This points to a strong family feeling. This time the suffering is not on the side of the Thessalonians but on that of Paul, and the unexpressed thought is that the presence of the Thessalonian brothers would have brought him solace.

We see something of this again when Paul says that he had been "encouraged" by the Thessalonians (1 Thess 3:7). He had been separated from them and did not know how they were doing; they had undergone some form of persecution, but how had they survived? It was an anxious time. But "brother Timothy" (1 Thess 2:2) came to Paul with news that the new converts were going on in the faith, and Paul was greatly cheered (1 Thess 2:6-8). If it was true that Paul was a great help to the young Christians, it was also true that these same young Christians were a great help to Paul. Membership in the family of God means helpfulness both ways.

Indeed others besides Paul had profited from the brotherly attitudes of the Thessalonian Christians. Paul had no need to write to them about brotherly love because God himself had taught these new members of his household (1 Thess 4:9; the word rendered "taught by God" is found only here in the New Testament). The result was that their loving helpfulness had gone out to all the Christians in Macedonia (1 Thess 4:9-10). Clearly the Thessalonian believers had learned that they were required to act in a brotherly way to others, as well as receive the blessing attendant on fellowship themselves.

Brotherhood also imposed obligations on Paul. Thus he says not simply, "we give thanks to God for you," but, "we ought to give thanks for you," "we owe it to give thanks for you," and he immediately adds, "as it is fitting" (2 Thess 1:3). He repeats the thought: "*we* ought always to give thanks to God for you, brothers beloved by the Lord" (2 Thess 2:13; "we" is emphatic); whatever the case with the others, *we* owe it as a duty to give thanks.

The letters give most attention to the obligations brotherhood imposes on the imperfectly instructed new believers at Thessalonica. Paul, however, does not overlook the fact that brotherhood imposes obligations on him, too. Paul sets a good example for us as well as for the early church. We find it easier to make strong criticisms of fellow Christians who do not act in the church as we think they should than to thank God for them all and for the varied contributions they bring to the family of God.

High standards

Paul strongly desires the best for his brothers and sisters, and in pursuit of this aim he addresses a strong exhortation to them ("we ask and exhort you in the Lord Jesus") that they "walk" in the way they had been instructed (1 Thess 4:1). He goes on to point to the importance of sanctification, and he emphasizes sexual purity, thus drawing attention to a standard very different from any commonly accepted in the Greek cities of the first century. Brotherhood does not mean complaisance, turning a blind eye to the faults of another. It means a deep and genuine concern for the prosperity of each other at every level. Among other things, it means reminding each other of the standards expected of Christians, whatever the standards in the surrounding environment.

Paul has a rather unexpected twist to his argument for sexual purity. As he develops his thought, he goes on to urge that none "go beyond and defraud his brother in the matter" (1 Thess 4:6). The point of this is that any brother or sister has the right to go into marriage with a chaste spouse. Anyone who prevents this, besides committing a sexual sin, is perpetrating an act of fraud—he or she is robbing his or her spouse of something that is rightfully to be expected (an aspect of sexual relationships not widely appreciated in our day).

6   THE CHRISTIAN LIFE

In this chapter we will look at a number of qualities to which Paul gives attention and which were important for the way those early Christians lived out their faith. For that matter, they are still important for those who are in earnest about their Christianity. There are qualities of character that set Christians off from those who do not profess the faith, and these had to be made clear to the Thessalonians. They had no long tradition of Christian service to follow; they were pioneers of the faith.

We owe much to early Christians like the Thessalonians. On the one hand, they had heard the gospel, and they put their trust in Christ. They knew what it was to have their sins forgiven and to pledge their loyalty to their Savior. On the other, they had no tradition of Christian service to observe, no host of godly Christian examples to follow. They were the first generation of humble, ordinary Christians who had had no contact with the saving events in Palestine. They had to work out what the Christian way meant for ordinary people.

It is perhaps for this reason that Paul unhesitatingly calls on them to imitate him. "For you know how you must imitate us," he writes (2 Thess 3:7), where his "must" should not be overlooked. It is not that all believers must be clones of Paul. It is rather that there were so few Christian examples for them to follow that it was *necessary*, not simply advisable, that they should follow those few examples that they had. Paul bore in mind that his example was important, as we see, for example, from the fact that he goes on to tell his readers that he and his associates had worked constantly to earn their living during the time when they evangelized Thessalonica. They did not do this because they did not have the right to be kept by those to whom they brought the gospel; they did have this right (1 Cor 9:14). They worked for their living "in order that we might give ourselves to you as a pattern so that you should imitate us" (2 Thess 3:9).

Early in his first letter, Paul reminds his readers that they had become "imitators of us and of the Lord" (1 Thess 1:6; cf. 1 Cor 11:1). It is perhaps a little unexpected that he puts the preachers in the first place in this expression, but historically this is the way it had to be. The preachers were the first contact these former heathen had had with Christianity, and when they committed themselves to follow Christ they necessarily followed him in the way their teachers showed them. They imitated the preachers in order that they might imitate Christ.

In time they found other models, and they became imitators of the churches in Judea (1 Thess 2:14). Those churches had experienced persecution before the Thessalonians did and thus set an example for other troubled churches to follow.

The Thessalonians must have often found themselves in situations for which they had no precedent. Believers like these were pioneers of the Christian way as it appears to ordinary, limited people, not to great people like Paul and Silvanus and Timothy. They sometimes got it right, and Paul praises them. If they got it wrong on other occasions, this was only to be expected, and we should be grateful to them for their blundering, first steps along the Christian path. We can learn from their successes, and we can learn from their failures, and we can learn from the instructions Paul gives and his comments on their spiritual state.

Sanctification

We tend to think of "holiness," "sanctification," and related words in terms of ethical achievement. A holy person, we think, is a good person. Now goodness is, of course, one of the qualities necessarily included in what Christians understand as a holy person. The basic idea, however, is not that; it is rather that of being set apart for God.

In Old Testament days when an object was sanctified, it was withdrawn from common use and set apart for use in the service of God. For example, when the tabernacle was set up in the wilderness, Moses was commanded to prepare a laver and sanctify (or consecrate) it (Exod 40:11). Previously it might have been used for all sorts of washings; after it was sanctified, it was to be used only in the service of God. Aaron and his sons were also sanctified (Exod 29:44); they became priests, set apart from other duties so that they belonged, in a particular way, to God.

Every Christian is to be sanctified, set apart to belong to God. This does not mean a physical separation from worldly people, but it does mean that the Christian life is a life lived for God, not for one's selfish concerns or for some human aim such as social or financial success, the service of the state, or the like.

Sanctification receives unusual attention in our two letters. The word itself occurs four times, whereas in the much longer letter to the Romans it is found only twice. The actual word count does not in itself indicate the precise

The Christian Life

emphasis Paul is giving to the concept, but it is an interesting pointer. Paul relates the term to sexual purity; he has the strong statement: "This is God's will, your sanctification, that you should abstain from fornication" (1 Thess 4:3). This is further developed: "that each of you should know to possess his own vessel in sanctification and honor, not in the lust of strong desire even as the Gentiles who do not know God" (vv 4–5). As we saw in an earlier chapter, Paul goes on to say that fornication is an act of fraud (robbing the future spouse of the chastity that spouse expects to be brought to the marriage relationship). He goes on to say, "For God did not call us on the basis of uncleanness, but in sanctification" (v 7). To despise this command then means not to despise a man, but God, the God who gives us his Holy Spirit (v 8).

The term occurs once in the second letter: "God chose you a firstfruit for salvation in sanctification of spirit (or of the Spirit) and belief of truth unto which he called us through our gospel" (2 Thess 2:13–14). Here sanctification is clearly seen as relevant to the whole of life.

All this means that the Christian life is a life not only initiated by God but sustained by God. The call of God is, of course, the primary thing (1 Thess 2:12; 5:24; 2 Thess 2:14); none of us would be Christians at all were it not for God's having called us. This call, however, is a call "in sanctification" (1 Thess 4:7), which surely means that sanctification is basic to the Christian way. Anyone who has been saved by God belongs to God, and God gives his Holy Spirit to those he calls in this way (v 8). Believers are not left to their own devices in seeking to serve God; divine strength and guidance are given them.

This appears to be what is in mind when Paul says that God chose the Thessalonians as a firstfruit for salvation "in sanctification of the Spirit" (2 Thess 2:13). Some exegetes have seen a reference to the human spirit, in which case the passage means that sanctification extends through the whole of the person, including his spirit. Yet it is much more likely that the apostle is saying that sanctification is not brought about by human striving. It is the Holy Spirit who works in and through people to make them the very people of God.

Either way, Paul is not talking about some placebo that leaves sinners basically where they were before. He is referring to a spiritual upheaval that transforms the whole person. Sanctification means the setting apart of all that a person is and has so that all now belongs to God.

We see this also in the closing prayer at the end of the first letter: "Now the God of peace himself sanctify you wholly, and may your entire spirit and soul and body be kept blameless at the coming of our Lord Jesus Christ. Faithful is he who has called you who also will do it" (1 Thess 5:23-24). Again Paul makes it clear that sanctification is the work of God, not of the believer; we are sanctified not by our strenuous efforts to live close to God, but by what God does in us as we respond to his gracious call.

In this passage there is also some emphasis on the far-reaching nature of sanctification with the use of the word "wholly," which surely points to the entire person. This is spelled out with the words "entire spirit and soul and body"; no part of us is left out. We are back at the priority of the divine when we read, "be kept blameless at the coming of our Lord Jesus Christ." The passive "be kept" points to something that is done for us, not to something that we do, and that we are to be blameless at the coming of the Lord Jesus shows that God's work in us will last to the very end. This truth is underlined with the assurance that God is "faithful" and that he who has called us "will do it" (cf. Phil 1:6). We can rely on God, who has begun a good work in us, to see it through to the end. With another word for sanctification, we have elsewhere the thought of being kept blameless at the parousia (1 Thess 3:13).

Part of Paul's teaching on sanctification is brought out with his use of the adjective "holy." He uses this, of course, for the "Holy Spirit," whom God gives to believers with the result that they are sanctified (1 Thess 4:8), as we have just seen. The apostle can also appeal to what happened when the gospel first came to the Thessalonians. "Our gospel did not come to you in word only," he writes, "but also in power and in the Holy Spirit and in full assurance" (1 Thess 1:5). The linking of the Spirit with the gospel and with power shows that Paul is not ascribing what happened in Thessalonica to powerful preaching or anything of the sort. He is referring to the power of God at work, transforming useless and fearful lives. There is a new power at work in those who have responded to the gospel, a power the Holy Spirit gives them.

With that goes assurance. Life always has its problems and uncertainties, and these can lead people to be worried and anxious. The Holy Spirit at work in them does not turn them into brash achievers, proud of their ability to cope, but the Spirit does give them assurance. Believers are assured that all of life is lived in the presence of God, the God who has a purpose for them and who will surely bring that purpose to pass. The Christian does not profess to be able to make sense of all life's tangled skein; believers do not claim to have fathomed the purpose of all that happens. Believers, however, know God, and therefore they know that there is a purpose, that the purpose is God's, and that it is God who understands how that purpose is to be worked out. To know this is to have "full assurance."

We have noticed references to the Holy Spirit's sanctifying work (1 Thess 5:23; 2 Thess 2:13). The Spirit also does other things, and we should bear in mind that Paul speaks of the converts as "having received the word in great affliction with joy of the Holy Spirit" (1 Thess 1:6). The trouble that the converts experienced was real, but so, too, was the presence of the Holy Spirit within them, and that Holy Spirit brought them joy. Neither the afflictions that are so much part and parcel of this common life nor those that are special, like the persecution the Thessalonians had experienced, can withstand the presence of the Spirit of God. The Spirit brought the believers joy, even in the midst of trouble.

"Do not quench the Spirit" (1 Thess 5:19) is an exhortation that raises problems. The word "quench" is used of putting out fires, and its suitability for acts in opposition to the Spirit is shown in that the Spirit came with what looked like "tongues of fire" (Acts 2:3; cf. Matt 3:11) and that the Spirit brings light and warmth to the life of the believer. Problems arise about precisely what activity is in mind here. Many commentators think there were conservative leaders who limited the enthusiastic use of ecstatic gifts, but this seems to be reading something into the passage; such gifts are not mentioned elsewhere in these letters. It is possible that it is prophecy that Paul has primarily in mind, for a reference to prophecy follows immediately, but the words about quenching are general, and it is likely that the apostle has in mind the truth that it is possible to oppose the Spirit by conduct like idleness, immorality, and the like. He may well be warning his readers against the loss of spiritual power and joy by engaging in any form of Spirit-quenching conduct.

Holy ones and holy actions

There are two passages where we read of "holy ones" at the time of Christ's *parousia*. The Lord Jesus will come "with all his holy ones" (1 Thess 3:13), and he will come "to be glorified in his holy ones" (2 Thess 1:10). We looked at those passages in our study of the last things and saw that they should be understood to refer to God's own people. They are those that God has sanctified and who are thus properly called "holy ones."

There are other passages that employ the word "holy." Thus Paul exhorts the Thessalonians that they should, "Greet all the brothers with a holy kiss" (1 Thess 5:26). Not much is known about kissing in the early church, but it is generally held that men kissed men and women kissed women during observances of the Lord's Supper (although Tertullian, at the end of the second century, speaks of a Christian wife kissing "one of the brothers"). Paul is asking that a warm greeting be given from him to all the members. That the kiss is "holy" points to it as part of the way the consecration of believers was worked out. This kiss is not the expression of passion, nor a mere conventional greeting, but a mark of warmth toward others set apart to belong to God.

Love

It has often been pointed out that Christians brought a new idea of love into the world. Whereas previously the best love had been a warm affection for someone or something one esteemed highly, the Christians saw in the cross, where the sinless Son of God died for sinners, the pattern of a new love (Rom 5:8; 1 John 4:10). "God is love," they said (1 John 4:8, 16), and this pointed to a love that proceeded from the nature of God, not from the nature of attractive objects. It is because God is the kind of God he is, a God who is love, that he loves sinners. He loves because of what he is, not because of what they are. Indeed, he loves them despite what they are, for to a pure and holy God there is nothing attractive about sinners.

When sinners respond to the love of God, they find that God's love remakes them. A new creation takes place (2 Cor 5:17), and they become loving people. They begin to love, not because the people they meet are attractive, but because God's love has also made them loving.

A number of times Paul brings out the truth that God loves the converts: they are "brothers beloved by God" (1 Thess 1:4) or "brothers beloved by the Lord" (2 Thess 2:13). In view of the close relationship between God the Father and the Lord Jesus Christ, it is not wise to try to put too big a difference between the two expressions; both affirm a strong divine love. There is an interesting problem when Paul links "our Lord Jesus Christ" with "God our Father" and follows with a pair of participles in the singular, "who loved us and gave us eternal encouragement and good hope in grace" (2 Thess 2:16). It is not certain whether we should see the Father as the subject of the participles or whether the Father and the Son are so closely linked that a verb referring to both can be singular. For our present purpose what matters is that we have another affirmation of the strong divine love that brought the good gifts of hope and grace.

In another little prayer Paul asks that the Lord may "direct your hearts into the love of God and into the steadfastness of Christ" (2 Thess 3:5). We would expect that in a prayer like this "the love of God" would mean the converts' love for God; we would think that Paul would be asking that the converts would come to love God more fully. Yet when the apostle uses the expression elsewhere, it has the meaning "God's love for people." It may well be that here he is bearing in mind the possibility of both meanings. The love of God for us is primary, and he may well be praying that the Thessalonians would respond to that love with an answering love. Then, when he goes on to steadfastness, he may well be thinking similarly of the steadfastness so typical of Christ and asking that such steadfastness will make its appearance in the believers.

While Christians, being loving people, will have a love for all, they will have a special affection for those who share with

The Christian Life

them in the common faith. So we find that the Thessalonian converts have been taught by God to love one another (1 Thess 4:9), and, so important is this love, it does not surprise us that Paul prays that the Lord will make the converts "increase and abound in love to one another and to all" (1 Thess 3:12).

The addition "and to all" is important; it shows clearly that Christian love is not confined to love within the fellowship. The love of one another is important, but it is important, too, that Christians not be self-centered, concentrating on affection within the church to the neglect of those outside the church. The people outside are yet within the scope of God's love and, therefore, of the love of those who love like God loves.

It is a matter of thanksgiving for Paul that "the love of each one of you all for one another abounds" (2 Thess 1:3). It is of interest that in the first letter he prayed that the love of the believers for one another should grow and now he is able to give thanks for the answer to that prayer. We are reminded that it is important not only that there be love, but that that love should grow.

In one instance Paul reminds them of distinctions within the community, namely, when he asks the believers to esteem their leaders "very highly in love for their work's sake" (1 Thess 5:13). It is easy to be critical of those in places of leadership, but Christians see their work as important, and for the sake of that work they regard them highly and they regard them with love. As love is to be characteristic of their relationship to other people, even those outside the church, much more should love be their attitude to those who lead within the church.

Right at the beginning of this correspondence, immediately after the greeting in the first letter, Paul gives thanks and prays for the Thessalonians "remembering your work of faith and labor of love" (1 Thess 1:3; he adds, "and steadfastness of hope"). "Labor" means more than the occasional kind deed; it points to hard work and brings out the truth that truly loving people are ready to go to great pains for others as the outworking of love.

In this passage faith is linked with love, and this happens a number of times in these letters (1 Thess 3:6; 5:8; 2 Thess 1:3). It is important that the two be seen to go together, for Paul is not writing of a love that people work up out of their own resources. It is a love that is the result of their responding to the love of God in Christ, and this response is a response in faith: they come to believe in Christ.

Just as we understand that love and faith are linked, so we must understand that love and holiness are connected. We see this in what Scripture says about God himself. God is love (1 John 4:8, 16) and God is also holy (Lev 11:45; Isa 6:3). The two qualities go together in the Godhead. This means (among other things) that God is opposed to every evil thing (see above, pp. 85–86). It means, too, that he is opposed to every evil in his beloved ones. Because he loves them, he wants the best for them, and he see that doing evil diminishes them.

We must accordingly take seriously his demand that believers live holy lives (1 Thess 4:3–8; so also Lev 11:45; 19:2). We must not understand the love of God as though it meant complaisance. The sentimental person claims to love others and because of this kind of "love" takes no strong measures against any evil the "loved one" may do. Not so God. We know his love because of the cross, the cross on which his Son died to put away our sin. All too often we let our understanding of the cross stop there, but we should never forget that the cross also shows us the seriousness with which God takes sin. In the light of the cross, those who really know the divine love cannot but have a horror of evil and a firm determination to live holy lives. Nothing motivates us to holiness like a right understanding of love.

The Christian Life

At the heart of Christianity is the faith that Jesus died and rose again (1 Thess 4:14) and "belief of the truth" (2 Thess 2:13) is fundamental; those who do not believe the truth face judgment (v 12). Not all men have faith (2 Thess 3:2), for some believe the lie (2 Thess 2:11). All who are saved have faith; they have put their trust in Christ.

Faith is the fundamental Christian attitude, and it is appropriate that Paul begins this correspondence by giving thanks for "your work of faith" (1 Thess 1:3). Faith, of course, means total reliance on God in Christ for salvation, but faith is not laziness. So Paul can pray that God will fulfill every "work of faith" in the Thessalonians (2 Thess 1:11). Faith will necessarily result in good works. Faith issues in work, not as leading to salvation, but as the outworking of salvation. The central importance of faith in the Christian life comes out in the way Christians are called simply "believers" (1 Thess 1:7; 2:10; 2 Thess 1:10, etc.). Furthermore, "the word of God" is active; it "works in you who believe" (1 Thess 2:13).

Thus in those early days when Paul was separated from the Thessalonians and could not bear the uncertainty about how they were progressing, he says, "We sent Timothy . . . to strengthen you and encourage you for the sake of your faith," and again, "I sent to know your faith" (1 Thess 3:2, 5). It was their faith that mattered. If that had collapsed all his work in the city was in vain. Timothy, however, brought him good news about their faith and love (v 6), and their faith was an encouragement to him (v 7). All this meant that their faith remained and that, therefore, they were still on the Christian path.

Even though his fears had been dispelled, Paul was still deeply concerned about the faith of his friends: "Night and day," he says, "praying exceedingly abundantly to see your face and perfect what is lacking in your faith" (1 Thess 3:10).

The earlier verses had reassured him that the Thessalonians were basically right, but they were still new Christians and there were deficiencies that could be made good and which Paul looks to see made good.

If he could pray that their faith might be made more perfect, when he comes to his second letter he can give thanks for the answer to that prayer: "We ought to give thanks to God always for you, brothers, even as it is fitting, because your faith is growing vigorously" (2 Thess 1:3). Clearly subsequent events showed that Paul's preliminary doubts about the faith of these converts had no real basis. They were going on in the faith, and their faith was growing. Indeed, Paul goes on to say that he and his companions boast about the Thessalonians in the churches of God "for your steadfastness and faith in all your persecutions" (v 4). Their faith was no fairweather faith. It proved steadfast during persecutions and afflictions.

Hope

It was apparently an early Christian habit to group faith, hope, and love together (1 Thess 1:3; 5:8; Rom 5:1–5; 1 Cor 13:13; Gal 5:5–6; Col 1:4–5; Heb 6:10–12; 10:22–24; 1 Pet 1:21–22). We are not surprised at finding faith on such a short list, for that is the basic Christian attitude. Nor do we wonder at love, for surely nothing is more important than living in love. But hope? In the modern world, along with the communities in which we live, we have mostly reduced hope to mindless optimism. Modern Christians have too often lost the blazing certainty that marked New Testament hope. We now relegate it to a minor place.

Hope, however, is important. No movement has really gripped the hearts of any considerable number of people that has not given them hope. It is no gain, but a considerable loss, if we let go of this significant New Testament teaching. The

New Testament Christians so emphasized hope that they could speak of Christ as their hope (1 Tim 1:1; cf. Col 1:27). They were saved in hope (Rom 8:24); hope was for them the anchor of the soul (Heb 6:18–19). By contrast, those who are without hope are faced with sorrow (1 Thess 4:13).

Hope was very important for the frequently downtrodden early believers. It is not surprising that the Thessalonian letters have some interesting things to say about hope. Thus Paul refers to "the steadfastness of your hope in our Lord Jesus Christ before our God and Father" (1 Thess 1:3). There is uncertainty as to whether the words about Christ and God refer to the previously mentioned faith and love as well as to hope, but none about their reference to hope. The Christian hope is bound up with what Christ has done for our salvation, and it is a hope exercised before God the Father. This is no idle emotion but rather a sterling quality, well based and exercised in the highest realms.

In an interesting passage Paul asks, "For what is our hope, or joy, or crown of rejoicing (are not you?) before our Lord Jesus at his coming?" (1 Thess 2:19). Something of his pride and joy in the Thessalonian converts comes through in this question, but it also implies his deep conviction that the hope that meant so much to him included the certainty that when the Lord Jesus comes back at the end of the age the Thessalonians will be there, sharing in the triumph and the joy of that great day. Hope is not exhausted by anything in the present.

Paul is fond of the metaphor of the Christian's armor, and he can speak of putting on a helmet, "the hope of salvation" (1 Thess 5:8). Hope looks right through this present life to the culmination of our salvation at our Lord's return. The helmet and the breastplate (which is here faith and love), are the two most important parts of defensive armor (which is all that Paul is concerned with in this place). When armed with faith, love, and hope, believers have all the armor they need. There is nothing more important for the Christian life than these.

Paul refers in a prayer to the divine gift of "eternal encouragement and good hope in grace" (2 Thess 2:16). This surely looks beyond this life to the eschatological fulfillment of the promises of God that means so much throughout these letters. The Christian's hope is for good things in this life certainly, but it looks also for the consummation of it all in the perfect kingdom of God.

The Christian Life

NOTES

Introduction
1. Abraham J. Malherbe, *Paul and the Thessalonians* (Philadelphia: Fortress, 1987), 17.
2. *New Testament Studies*, 17 (1970-71), 449-50.

Chapter 1   The Living and True God
1. D. E. H. Whiteley can say, "Perhaps the most striking feature of both epistles is the pervasiveness of the sense of God and His providence" (*Thessalonians* [London: Oxford University Press, 1969], 19).

Chapter 2   Jesus Christ Our Lord
1. Alfred Edersheim, *The Life and Times of Jesus the Messiah* (London: Longmans, Green and Co., 1890), 2: 710-41.
2. William Neil, *The Epistles of Paul to the Thessalonians* (London: Hodder and Stoughton, 1950), 185.
3. A. L. Moore, *1 and 2 Thessalonians*, New Century Bible (London: Nelson, 1969), 109-10.

Chapter 3   The Last Things
1. J. B. Lightfoot, *Notes on Epistles of St Paul* (London: Macmillan, 1904), 66.

2. C. K. Barrett, *A Commentary on the First Epistle to the Corinthians* (London: A. and C. Black, 1978), 5.

3. J. E. Frame, *A Critical and Exegetical Commentary on the Epistles of St. Paul to the Thessalonians* (Edinburgh: T. & T. Clark, 1960), 174.

4. William Hendriksen, *New Testament Commentary: Exposition of I and II Thessalonians* (Grand Rapids, Mich.: Baker, 1955), 116–17.

5. J. H. Moulton and G. Milligan, *The Vocabulary of the Greek Testament* (London: Hodder and Stoughton, 1914–29), 53.

6. W. Bauer, *A Greek-English Lexicon of the New Testament and Other Early Christian Literature*, trans. W. F. Arndt and F. W. Gingrich, 2d ed., rev. F. W. Gingrich and F. W. Danker (Chicago: University of Chicago Press, 1979), 564.

Chapter 4   The Defeat of Evil

1. Oscar Cullmann, *Christ and Time* (London: SCM, 1951), 164.

2. Ronald A. Ward, *Commentary on 1 & 2 Thessalonians* (Waco, Tex.: Word Books, 1973), 11.

Chapter 5   The Christian Family

1. When the New Testament writers refer to people as "beloved by God," they usually employ the adjective *agapētos* but Paul has here the participle *ēgapēmenoi*, the only place in the New Testament where this construction is used (although 2 Thess 2:13 and Jude 1 are very similar). Perhaps we can say that the perfect participle here puts some emphasis on God's continuing love.

INDEX OF SCRIPTURES